Progress in IS

More information about this series at http://www.springer.com/series/10440

Alexander Scheerer

Coordination in Large-Scale Agile Software Development

Integrating Conditions and Configurations
in Multiteam Systems

 Springer

Alexander Scheerer
SAP SE
Walldorf, Baden-Württemberg
Germany

ISSN 2196-8705   ISSN 2196-8713   (electronic)
Progress in IS
ISBN 978-3-319-85629-2   ISBN 978-3-319-55327-6   (eBook)
DOI 10.1007/978-3-319-55327-6

This book is based on a doctoral thesis successfully defended at the Business School of the University of Mannheim.

Printed on acid-free paper

This Springer imprint is published by Springer Nature
The registered company is Springer International Publishing AG
The registered company address is: Gewerbestrasse 11, 6330 Cham, Switzerland

The original version of the book was revised:
For detailed information please see erratum.
The erratum to this book is available at
DOI 10.1007/978-3-319-55327-6_6

Acknowledgements

This dissertation is the result of a successful cooperation between the research group of Prof. Dr. Armin Heinzl at the Institute of Enterprise Systems, University of Mannheim, Germany and SAP SE, Walldorf, Germany. Developing and writing this book has been a challenging and enriching experience. I would like to thank many people who have supported and accompanied me during this process.

First and foremost, I would like to thank my academic advisor Prof. Dr. Armin Heinzl for giving me the support, the guidance and also the freedom to develop my research ideas and skills in teaching. I deeply appreciate his encouragement and support to present at international conferences and to develop my work during a research stay abroad with Dr. Rashina Hoda at the University of Auckland.

This dissertation project would not have been possible without the amazing support I received from colleagues at SAP SE. Through innumerable discussions, interviews and workshops I had the unique opportunity to study agile software development with and from experts in the field. My special thanks goes to Tobias Schimmer (né Hildenbrand), who has been invaluable in this research endeavor. He has always been an encouraging and highly supportive mentor throughout this journey. Martin Fassunge, Juergen Heymann, Michael Römer and Joachim Schnitter guided me through the world of software development at SAP SE. Without their support, the successful completion of this joint research project would not have been possible. Furthermore, I would like to thank Behnaz Gholami, Herbert Illgner, Roger Kilian-Kehr, Günter Pecht-Seibert, Felix Maximilian Roth, Sarah Träutlein and Dirk Völz at SAP SE for their support. Furthermore, the empirical study would not have been possible without the support of more than 90 colleagues who were willing to be interviewed for my research on top of their daily work.

While working on my dissertation, I had the opportunity to collaborate with a great team of colleagues at the Chair of General Management and Information Systems. The ongoing exchanges about our work and beyond was all-important to this journey. Through this time spent together I was fortunate enough to have gained many a friend. My very special thanks goes to Okan Aydingül, Saskia Bick, Jens Förderer, Erik Hemmer, Lars Klimpke, Tommi Kramer, Thomas Kude,

Miroslav Lazic, Nele Lüker, Tillmann Neben, Marko Nöhren, Sven Scheibmayr, Kai Spohrer, Christoph Schmidt, Sebastian Stuckenberg and Aliona von der Trenck. I would also like to thank the chair's assistants Luise Bühler and Ingrid Distelrath as well as the student assistants, Stefan Eckhardt, Alexandra Lang, Lea Offermann and Martin Pfannemüller.

My deepest gratitude goes to my family, who have given me the utmost of encouragement and advice, especially to Saskia for her unceasing patience and my parents, who have always given me unconditional support in all aspects of life.

Mannheim, Germany   Alexander Scheerer
December 2016

Contents

Abbreviations

APO	Area Product Owner
Arch	Architect
CPO	Chief Product Owner
DSDM	Dynamic Systems Development Method
IC	Integrating Condition
IS	Information Systems
IT	Information Technology
LeSS	Large-Scale Scrum Framework
MTS	Multiteam System
PO	Product Owner
RUP	Rational Unified Process
SAFe	Scaled Agile Framework
SM	Scrum Master
UI	User Interface
XP	Extreme Programming

List of Figures

List of Tables

Chapter 1
Introduction

Software is like entropy. It is difficult to grasp, weighs nothing, and obeys the second law of thermodynamics; i.e. it always increases.

—Norman Ralph Augustine

1.1 Problem Statement

Software has permeated every aspect of modern life. Human kind flew to the moon on 140,000 lines of source code[1] and yet, when you wake up in the morning and put on your smartwatch, more than 10 million lines of code have just been strapped to your wrist. The same goes for the smartphone that happens to be buried somewhere in your bag; 12+ million lines of code in your pocket. The plane on route to your vacation destination will be hurling you and 14+ million lines of code through the air. These magnitudes are already impressing, and yet a quick 'like' on your favorite social network will be powered by 61+ million lines of code[2] and the pair of socks you have just bought at the retailer of your choice will fire off data into an enterprise system consisting of more than 400 million lines of code.[3] To put these numbers into perspective, one million lines of code printed out, would cover 18,000 pages and equals about 14 copies of War and Peace.[4] The development of such massive and complex software involves equally substantial and complex organizations whose members need to be carefully coordinated.

For a long time, the prevalent approach to develop large software products has been to minimize risk by intense upfront planning and rigid stage-gated processes and structures. As the years went by, this led to a long time-to-market and inflexible requirements management, which prevented quick reactions to changing customer wishes (Mackert et al. 2010).

---

[1]http://www.itworld.com/article/2725085/big-data/curiosity-about-lines-of-code.html.
[2]http://www.informationisbeautiful.net/visualizations/million-lines-of-code/.
[3]http://blogs.gartner.com/robert-anderson/2015/06/10/musings-sapphire-now-2015/.
[4]War and Peace by Leo Tolstoy, first published in 1869 with 1225 pages.

© Springer International Publishing AG 2017
A. Scheerer, *Coordination in Large-Scale Agile Software Development*,
Progress in IS, DOI 10.1007/978-3-319-55327-6_1

The introduction of more lightweight development methods in the middle of the 1990s can be seen as a countermovement to this very heavyweight approach. Their flexibility and adaptability has let them become a de facto standard in large parts of many software organizations of different sizes (VersionOne Inc. 2012; West et al. 2010).

As the origins of agile development lie in small settings with a limited amount of developers, many of these approaches have been regarded in light of small companies, single team settings, or student developer teams. However, these development methods have increasingly gained prominence in large-scale settings as well (e.g. Begel and Nagappan 2007; Fry and Greene 2007; Nerur et al. 2005). When moving into the context of large development efforts, new challenges specific to those settings arise as the higher number of people contributing to these large development projects need to be carefully coordinated (Shepperd 1993). Such development efforts usually follow the general movement in new product development of team-based organizations (Kozlowski and Bell 2003) and result in a team of teams setup (Larman and Vodde 2008), where several teams have to work together on a single software product.

This organizational setup has been defined as a multiteam system (MTS), which is a setting of multiple teams working jointly and interdependently towards collective goals (Mathieu et al. 2001).

Literature on coordination would suggest a more top-down planning approach to coordination in such large-scale settings (cf. Van De Ven et al. 1976). Yet, agile development methods focus on a strong bottom-up adjustment style of coordination. The combination of these two opposing strategies seems contradicting. Nonetheless, the primarily knowledge-intensive tasks in software development must be coordinated across different organizational levels, which includes bottom-up approaches to make use of specialized knowledge and top-down strategies to create efficiency within the system. One the one hand, this clearly calls for a setting where both coordination strategies are necessary. On the other hand, however, two shortcomings become evident.

First, the two mentioned coordination approaches are often presented as two stereotypes, which in fact represent the two extremes of a broad spectrum, combinations of which have barely been looked at. Second, the classical coordination approaches are usually viewed as static or situational characteristics of a (multi-team) system, despite the fact that these coordination mechanisms are being applied over time. For example, in a bottom-up approach to coordination teams apply certain collaborative and iterative methods and tools to provide feedback to higher organizational levels as well as to their collaborating teams and thereby actually undergo a time-dependent process of coordination. That is, the applied coordination approach within a system of actors is conceptualized as a characterization of this system, rather than seen as a dynamic process of change. Conceptualizing coordination as a change process, which can, if answering a disruptive situation, make use of several different coordination mechanisms depending on the environmental situation, is a view independent of a system's basic coordination strategy.

The call for more research on inter-team coordination in large-scale agile software development systems has only recently started to emerge. Dingsøyr and Moe (2013, 2014) present a research agenda with the topic of inter-team coordination ranked as number one. This research intends to answer their call and shed light on coordination in large-scale agile software development.

1.2 Research Questions and Objectives

Previous studies revealed that a thorough theoretical understanding in the field of agile software development is lacking and have called for more studies on the underlying fundamental concepts in this field (Abrahamsson et al. 2009; Ågerfalk et al. 2009; Dybå and Dingsøyr 2008). More precisely, there is not only a lack of research on large-scale agile software development in general and the ongoing processes in particular, but there is also close to no research on coordination on an inter-team level which has led to several calls for research (Dingsøyr and Moe 2013, 2014). To characterize the existing coordination processes in these multiteam systems, a coordination configuration was developed with the dimensions coordination type, locus and direction. The enactment of a specific coordination configuration enables the emergence of particular integrating conditions for coordinated action, which in turn leads to a state of coordinated action. This research project intends to advance the understanding of coordination in agile multiteam software development systems by answering the central research question via two sub questions:

> How do changes in the coordination configuration affect the integrating conditions for coordination in multiteam software development systems?
>
> (1) Why does the coordination configuration change?
> (2) How are the integrating conditions for coordination attained?

The results that aim to answer these research questions are expected to be of interest for both research and practice. This study is among the first to investigate large agile multiteam software development systems from a coordination perspective and thereby seeks to substantially advance the understanding of inter-team coordination in large-scale agile settings (Dingsøyr and Moe 2013, 2014). In doing so, this study seeks to contribute to the two main areas described above: large-scale agile software development and inter-team coordination. By examining different multiteam systems in the field, this study shall improve the understanding of different scaling approaches within large-scale agile software development in real life settings. Among the studies on coordination, this research is one of the first to investigate the underlying factors, which are considered to be necessary conditions for coordinated action. In regarding these conditions that separate the mechanisms of coordination from the coordinated action they achieve, a deeper understanding of detailed coordination processes and the inherent process changes is sought. Finally, the study results should provide practitioners with a guideline to evaluate coordination practices in large-scale agile development settings and act as a foundation for evidence-based management of software products.

1.3 Research Design and Organization

This study follows a qualitative case study approach (Eisenhardt 1989) sometimes referred to as soft positivism (Kirsch 2004; Madill et al. 2000). This allowed the data analysis to be performed with certain expectations based on prior theory, but at the same time permitted unexpected results and explanations to be derived from the data, an approach closer to the interpretivist paradigm.

Research in the field of agile software development is considered to be at an intermediate state (Dybå and Dingsøyr 2008). Based on this assessment, a qualitative case study approach (Yin 2009) seems particularly fitting as the research phenomenon is not supported by a strong theoretical base (Benbasat et al. 1987). Similarly, Edmondson and McManus (2007) suggest an exploratory qualitative approach for research areas in a nascent theoretical state.

The research is structured along two stages (see Fig. 1.1). In the first stage, a deductive approach was taken through a review of the literature on coordination and agile development, which led to the construction of a research framework. In the second stage, a multiple case study was conducted with a process theoretical approach (Markus and Robey 1988; Mohr 1982) as this research project intends to achieve more explanatory power through a time-based view. In line with Lyytinen and Newman (2006, 2008), who propose interviews, observations and document analysis as principal data collection for process models, an exploratory multiple case study with five MTSs and a total of 66 interviewees was undertaken.

This thesis is structured into five main chapters. Having introduced the study in the current chapter, Chapter 2 presents the foundations of coordination research, teams and multiteam systems, agile software development and prior work on

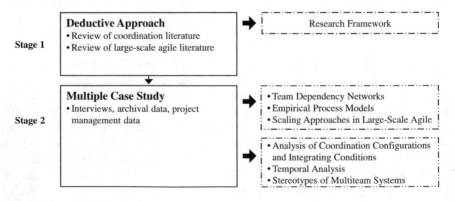

Fig. 1.1 Research Organization

coordination in multiteam systems, as well as large-scale agile development that act as the groundwork from which the research framework is constructed. Chapter 3 describes the context of this study as well as the employed research data collection and analysis methods used herein. Chapter 4 provides the findings of the multiple case study conducted, starting with the single-case and continuing with the cross-case analyses of the five cases. Chapter 5 summarizes the study results and discusses the theoretical and practical contributions. This last chapter closes with limitations and future work as well as the concluding remarks.

References

Abrahamsson, P., Conboy, K., & Wang, X. (2009). "Lots done, more to do": The current state of agile systems development research. *European Journal of Information Systems, 18*(4), 281–284. Retrieved from http://www.palgrave-journals.com/ejis/journal/v18/n4/abs/ejis200927a.html

Ågerfalk, P. J., Fitzgerald, B., & Slaughter, S. (2009). Flexible and distributed information systems development: State of the art and research challenges. *Information Systems Research, 20*(3), 317–328.

Begel, A., & Nagappan, N. (2007). Usage and perceptions of agile software development in an industrial context: An exploratory study. In *International Symposium on Empirical Software Engineering and Measurement* (pp. 255–264). IEEE Computer Society. Retrieved from http://doi.ieeecomputersociety.org/10.1109/ESEM.2007.12

Benbasat, I., Goldstein, D. K., & Mead, M. (1987). The case research strategy in studies of information systems. MIS Quarterly, *11*(3).

Dingsøyr, T., & Moe, N. B. (2013). Research challenges in large-scale agile software development. *ACM SIGSOFT Software Engineering Notes, 38*(5), 38–39. Retrieved from http://dl.acm.org/citation.cfm?id=2507288.2507322

Dingsøyr, T., & Moe, N. B. (2014). Towards principles of large-scale agile development. In T. Dingsøyr, N. Moe, R. Tonelli, S. Counsell, C. Gencel, & K. Petersen (Eds.), *Agile methods. Large-scale development, refactoring, testing, and estimation* (Vol. 199, pp. 1–8). Springer International Publishing. Retrieved from http://www.springer.com/computer/swe/book/978-3-319-14357-6

Dybå, T., & Dingsøyr, T. (2008). Empirical studies of agile software development: A systematic review. *Information and Software Technology, 50*(9–10), 833–859. Retrieved from http://linkinghub.elsevier.com/retrieve/pii/S0950584908000256

Edmondson, A. C., & McManus, S. E. (2007). Methodological fit in management field research. *The Academy of Management Review, 32*(4), 1155–1179.

Eisenhardt, K. M. (1989). Building theories from case study research. *The Academy of Management Review, 14*(4), 532–550. Retrieved from http://www.jstor.org/stable/258557

Fry, C., & Greene, S. (2007). Large scale agile transformation in an on-demand world. In *Proceedings of the AGILE Conference 2007* (pp. 136–142). Washington, DC.

Kirsch, L. J. (2004). Deploying common systems globally: The dynamics of control. *Information Systems Research, 15*(4), 374–395.

Kozlowski, S. W. J., & Bell, B. S. (2003). Work groups and teams in organizations. In W. C. Borman, D. R. Ilgen, & R. J. Klimoski (Eds.), *Handbook of psychology: Industrial and organizational psychology* (Vol. 12, pp. 333–375). New York: Wiley.

Larman, C., & Vodde, B. (2008). *Scaling lean & agile development: Thinking and organizational tools for large-scale Scrum.* Upper Saddle River, NJ: Addison-Wesley Professional.

Lyytinen, K., & Newman, M. (2006). Working papers on information systems punctuated equilibrium, process models and information system development and change : Towards a socio-technical process analysis. *Sprouts: Working Papers on Information Systems*, *6*(2006), 1–49. Retrieved from http://sprouts.aisnet.org/46/1/060101_.pdf

Lyytinen, K., & Newman, M. (2008). Explaining information systems change: A punctuated socio-technical change model. *European Journal of Information Systems*, *17*(6), 589–613. Retrieved from http://www.palgrave-journals.com/ejis/journal/v17/n6/abs/ejis200850a.html

Mackert, O., Hildenbrand, T., & Podbicanin, A. (2010). Vom Projekt zum Produkt - SAP's Weg zum "Lean Software Product Development." In *Vom Projekt zum Produkt. Fachtagung des GI-Fachausschusses Management der Anwendungsentwicklung und -wartung im Fachbereich Wirtschaftsinformatik (WI-MAW), 01.-03. Dezember 2010 in Aachen* (pp. 13–25).

Madill, A., Jordan, A., & Shirley, C. (2000). Objectivity and reliability in qualitative analysis: Realist, contextualist and radical constructionist epistemologies. *British Journal of Psychology*, *91*(1), 1–20. Retrieved from http://dx.doi.org/10.1348/000712600161646

Markus, M. L., & Robey, D. (1988). Information technology and organizational change: Causal structure in theory and research. *Management Science*, *34*(5), 583–598. Retrieved from http://www.jstor.org/stable/10.2307/2632080

Mathieu, J. E., Marks, M. A., & Zaccaro, S. J. (2001). Multiteam systems. In N. Anderson, D. S. Ones, H. K. Sinangil, & C. Viswesvaran (Eds.), *Handbook of industrial, work and organizational psychology, Volume 2 Organizational psychology* (Vol. 2, pp. 289–313). London: Sage Publications Ltd.

Mohr, L. B. (1982). *Explaining organizational behavior*. San Francisco: Jossey-Bass.

Nerur, S. P., Mahapatra, R. K., & Mangalaraj, G. (2005). Challenges of migrating to agile methodologies. *Communications of the ACM*, *48*(5), 72–78.

Shepperd, J. a. (1993). Productivity loss in performance groups: A motivation analysis. *Psychological Bulletin*, *113*(1), 67–81.

Van De Ven, A. H., Delbecq, A. L., & Koenig, R. J. (1976). Determinants of coordination modes within organizations. *American Sociological Review*, *41*(2), 322–338. Retrieved from http://www.jstor.org/stable/2094477

VersionOne Inc. (2012). 7th Annual State of Agile Development Survey. Retrieved from http://www.versionone.com/pdf/7th-Annual-State-of-Agile-Development-Survey.pdf

West, D., Grant, T., Gerush, M., & D'Silva, D. (2010). Agile development: Mainstream adoption has changed agility. *Forrester Research*.

Yin, R. K. (2009). *Case study research: Design and methods* (4th ed.). Sage Publications, Inc.

Chapter 2
Theoretical and Conceptual Foundations

The theoretical foundations outline extant literature on coordination as well as on agile software development. To provide a basis for agile development on a large scale, first the underlying core concepts of coordination and agile software development on a small scale are presented before delving into prior work on coordination in multiteam systems and large-scale agile software development.

2.1 Coordination

Coordination is a multi-faceted research area, which takes its inputs from a variety of fields including but not limited to organizational theory and teamwork studies. Before the following chapter gives an overview of the different facets of coordination, different definitions of coordination will be discussed.

Across the different fields, there exist many definitions of coordination. Table 2.1 gives an overview. While covering a wide array of research interests, three common aspects within the definitions become apparent. The first refers to the *actors* who need to work together, the second being the *work*, which is interdependent, and thirdly a *goal* in the form of a piece of work, which is achieved (Okhuysen and Bechky 2009). In the context of software development, coordination can be viewed as the establishment of common understanding on what should be built, how to build it as well as alignment and integrating activities (Kraut and Streeter 1995). In its purest form, coordination is the "achievement of concerted action" (Kotlarsky et al. 2008, p. 96). It is this definition that will be adopted in this work.

© Springer International Publishing AG 2017
A. Scheerer, *Coordination in Large-Scale Agile Software Development*,
Progress in IS, DOI 10.1007/978-3-319-55327-6_2

Table 2.1 Definitions of coordination

Definition	Authors
Coordination is the achievement of concerted action	Kotlarsky et al. (2008, p. 96) citing Goodhue and Thompson (1995)
Coordination means integrating or linking together different parts of an organization to accomplish a collective set of tasks	Van De Ven et al. (1976, p. 322)
Coordination is managing dependencies between activities	Malone and Crowston (1994, p. 90)
Different people working on a common project agree to a common definition of what they are building, share information, and mesh their activities	Kraut and Streeter (1995, p. 69)
A temporally unfolding and contextualized process of input regulation and interaction articulation to realize a collective performance	Faraj and Xiao (2006, p. 1157)

2.1.1   Coordination in Organizational Theory

The study of coordination in organizational theory has a long and rich history. In the classical work from March and Simon (1958), the two prominent schools of thought of the time are presented: scientific management (Taylor 1911) and the administrative management school (Gulick and Urwick 1937). Scientific management deals with the analysis and management of workflows, especially of routine production tasks, and seeks to create prescribed operating procedures for effectiveness in organizations (Tosi 2008). The departmentalization model of the administrative school seeks to achieve organizational goals by examining how to organize jobs into components within the organization (e.g. grouping by common purpose or by common processes).

March and Simon (1958) criticized both streams because of their lack of appreciation for the human factor. They distinguished two main types of coordination: (1) coordination by plan and (2) coordination by feedback. In standardized and repetitive situations, the tasks become "programmable" through scheduling and are thus best coordinated by plan. If the circumstances require the diffusion of new information, coordination by feedback seems better suited. Feedback, being based on communication between employees, is also seen as a way to deal with deviations from the plan (March and Simon 1958).

Several years later, Thompson (1967) published his seminal work in which he cites March and Simon (1958) and presents three generic forms how coordination can be achieved. Based on the type of interdependence, an appropriate method of coordination is proposed. Three types of interdependencies are illustrated, (1) *pooled* or general, (2) *sequential* and (3) *reciprocal*. The pooled dependency, being the least coupled of all, arises when units within an organization accomplish completely separate tasks and do not need to interact. In the end, each business unit performs its part in the overall picture of the organization, which creates an implicit dependency to the other entities. The second dependency type, sequential, arises when one unit depends on the output of another to continue its work. A typical example for this is the production assembly line, where each consecutive step needs the input from the previous one. Finally, reciprocal dependency is the strongest form of coupling and occurs when input and output flow in both directions simultaneously between the dependent units (Thompson 1967).

Thompson (1967) suggests an appropriate coordination style for each type of task interdependency. As such, a pooled or generalized interdependence should be coordinated by *standardization* with little communication and decision effort. The sequential dependency type is best coordinated by *planning* and requires medium effort for communication and decision-making. The final type of dependency, reciprocal, should be coordinated by *mutual adjustment*, which is based on March and Simon's (1958) coordination by *feedback*. This coordination type is most challenging with regards to communication and decision efforts (Thompson 1967).

Van De Ven et al. (1976) considered three modes of coordination based on the work of March and Simon (1958) and Thompson (1967), namely *impersonal*, *personal* and *group* coordination. They argue that all coordination types in the form of programming, e.g. plans, rules and hierarchies (see Kieser 1993), can be grouped in the impersonal mode. The feedback or mutual adjustment type can be divided into personal and group modes, depending on the number of people involved. Furthermore, the personal mode includes either horizontal or vertical channels, up or down the hierarchy or across hierarchical levels, through which communication occurs. The group mode can be split into scheduled or unscheduled meetings of several people. In their study, Van De Ven et al. (1976) identified which factors influence the choice of coordination mechanisms. Three factors were chosen: *task uncertainty, task interdependence* and *size of work unit* (i.e. number of people employed in a work unit). They found that higher task uncertainty leads to higher use of mutual adjustment through horizontal channels and group meetings. With rising task interdependence, the amount of coordination mechanisms across all three modes rises as well. Finally, a higher unit size induces the use of more impersonal modes in the form of plans.

Mintzberg (1980) introduces five coordination mechanisms: (1) *direct supervision*, (2) *standardization of work processes*, (3) *standardization of outputs*, (4) *skills* and (5) *mutual adjustment*. Coordination via direct supervision entails one individual giving specific orders to others and thereby ensuring coordination. Standardization of work processes involves the regulation of how the work is done by rules or regulations, while the standardization of outputs specifies performance measures or work outputs. Through a set of standard expertise and knowledge, the standardization of skills is achieved. Finally, coordination by mutual adjustment includes communication by informal means among people (Mintzberg 1980). Concerning the location of coordination within organizations, Mintzberg (1980) advances the concept of *centralization* or *decentralization* of decision making within the firm boundaries as a key determinant of organizational structure.

This chapter has reviewed key works in organizational theory relating to coordination and the mechanisms used to achieve it. The next chapter will delve deeper into what is known as coordination theory (Malone and Crowston 1990, 1994).

2.1.2 Coordination Theory

Proposed by Malone and Crowston (1990), the main focus of their work lies on the analysis of coordination with respect to actors, interdependent activities and goals (Malone and Crowston 1994). The naming of this stream of literature is misleading, as the work published does not conform to the longstanding discussion on what constitutes a theory (Bacharach 1989; Sutton and Staw 1995). Bacharach (1989) pointed out based on Hempel (1965), that "the vocabulary of science has two basic functions: (a) to adequately describe the objects and events being investigated and (b) to establish theories by which events and objects can be explained and predicted" (Bacharach 1989, p. 496). While the work published on this topic (cf. Malone et al. 2003; Malone and Crowston 1991, 1994) can be seen as fulfilling function (a) since it describes dependency types and in parts how these interdependencies should be coordinated, no predictive power arises as no hypotheses or propositions are stated.

The types of dependencies considered by Malone et al. (1999) exist between resources and activities. Three basic types of dependencies that ensue from resources being associated with multiple activities are defined. The fit dependency occurs when several activities collectively produce a single resource. The manufacturing industry shows several examples of such dependencies, e.g. the production of cars or planes where several components need to be integrated to eventually form a complete product. The flow dependency occurs whenever a resource is produced by one activity, which is then the input to another. According to Malone et al. (1999), the flow dependency is comprised of three different kinds of constraints, a prerequisite, an accessibility and a usability constraint. All of these dependencies must be managed for a flow dependency, e.g. the right thing (usability) needs to be in the right place (accessibility) at the right time (prerequisite). Finally, a sharing dependency arises when several activities all use the same resource, i.e. the use of the same machine in several production processes.

More examples of dependency types that are given by Malone and Crowston (1994) are listed in Table 2.2. Here, the producer-consumer dependency is

Table 2.2 Dependencies and examples of coordination processes

Dependency	Examples of coordination processes
Producer-consumer (flow)	Sequencing and tracking for prerequisite constraints Inventory management for accessibility constraints Standardization for usability constraints
Task-subtask	Goal selection, goal decomposition

Based on Malone and Crowston (1994)

characterized by an activity producing a resource that is consumed by another activity, essentially the same as a flow dependency mentioned earlier. Exemplary coordination processes for managing such a dependency are sequencing and tracking for a prerequisite constraint, an inventory management for the accessibility constraint and lastly standardization for the usability constraint.

Malone and Crowston (1994) propose that the management of task-subtask dependencies can be achieved by the coordination processes goal selection and decomposition. An often found dependency, the task-subtask dependency, represents a situation where an overall goal includes a group of subtasks, which need to be completed in order to achieve the higher goal. A top-down goal decomposition can be utilized to manage task-subtask dependencies. Although this type of dependency is usually managed through a sequential process of goal selection and decomposition, it is entirely possible that a bottom-up identification of goals is achieved when employees recognize that tasks they are doing or new ideas they have could lead to new goals in line with the overall goal (Malone and Crowston 1994).

As mentioned earlier, no predictive or explanatory power arises from this work. In its current state it is deemed more of a pattern model (Crowston et al. 2006). Furthermore, issues of context and time are not taken into consideration. The diverse range of previous work on the topic of coordination (cf. Okhuysen and Bechky 2009) shows the necessity to include the context into any contemplation on the subject. Especially aspects of time are of great significance, as coordination is considered to be a temporally enfolding phenomenon (see Table 2.1).

Within the area of team cognition studies, coordination of individual team members has been a long-standing topic of interest. In the next chapter, aspects of coordination within this research stream will be presented.

2.1.3 Coordination in Team Cognition Studies

Within the research field of team cognition studies, which covers established concepts such as shared mental models or transactive memory systems within teams, the coordination modes have been subdivided into *explicit* and *implicit* coordination styles (Espinosa et al. 2004). The previously presented coordination modes in organizational theory are considered to be explicit in that they are carried out deliberately to coordinate groups in order to achieve a state of coordination. Implicit coordination on the other hand, is a mode of coordination that arises as a consequence of other acts and is used without the intention to coordinate. An example of this type is the often mentioned "water cooler" talk, i.e. informal exchanges of information between colleagues that nevertheless lead to better coordination.

Espinosa et al. (2010) present a taxonomy of coordination types including, mechanistic, organic and cognitive coordination. The first two originate from organizational theory as presented in Sect. 2.1.1, with cognitive coordination arising from research on team cognition. While *mechanistic coordination* includes coordination by plan or rules with little communication, *organic coordination* refers to coordination by means of mutual adjustment or feedback via interaction. This communication can be formal and planned or informal and spontaneous. *Cognitive coordination*, on the other hand, is based on tacit team knowledge the actors have about each other and is achieved implicitly (Rico et al. 2008).

Shared mental models (Cannon-Bowers et al. 1993) and transactive memory systems (Moreland et al. 1996) are two examples of cognitive or implicit coordination mechanisms (Espinosa et al. 2004). Shared mental models are the "common or overlapping cognitive representations of task requirements, procedures and role responsibilities" (Cannon-Bowers et al. 1993, p. 222). The transactive memory system contains the knowledge embedded in each person individually and a metamemory about the expertise domains of the other participants in this system (Moreland et al. 1996). While shared mental models represent a shared understanding between actors, transactive memory systems conceptualize the aspect of knowing who knows what. The shared mental model construct is central to teamwork, as it acts as a facilitator for the teams' goal focus and contributes to common understanding and action (Salas et al. 2005).

While this stream of coordination research proposes team cognition constructs as coordination mechanisms, the question remains what tangible coordination activity takes place. As the implicit nature of these types suggests, no overt coordination activity is observable. As such, these constructs may be viewed as traits, which lead to a reduction of mechanistic coordination, or even as conditions necessary for coordinated action.

2.1.4 Outcomes and Conditions of Coordination

After decades of research in the organizational domain (cf. Mintzberg 1983; Thompson 1967; Van De Ven et al. 1976), recent advances on the conditions and outcomes of coordination have been made outside of this field, namely in the areas of team cognition (cf. Cannon-Bowers et al. 1993; Moreland et al. 1996) and information systems (cf. Pikkarainen et al. 2008; Strode et al. 2012). The following section summarizes research on outcomes and conditions of coordination.

From the definitions of coordination in Table 2.1 it can be deduced that coordination can be conceptualized in two ways. Kotlarsky et al. (2008, p. 96) view coordination as "the achievement of concerted action", which depicts coordination as a state that is achieved, similarly to Lawrence and Lorsch (1967) who view coordination as a state to be attained. By contrast, Faraj and Xiao (2006, p. 1157) or Malone and Crowston (1994, p. 90) describe it as the management of dependencies or the "contextualized process of input regulation and interaction articulation", which expresses coordination as a process. In the end, it can be understood either as the process necessary to achieve concerted action or as the state that is achieved by this process.

Both coordination as a process and coordinated action as state are regarded as central aspects in achieving an overarching performance measure. The positive influence of coordination on performance measures has been widely recognized throughout literature (cf. Cheng 1984; Faraj and Xiao 2006; Kozlowski and Bell 2003; Nidumolu 1995; Simon 1976). As such, Cheng (1984, p. 830) describes coordination as "a necessary condition for effective organizational performance", however it is not sufficient by itself. Within the domain of team research, Kozlowski and Bell (2003, p. 353) state that previous "empirical research has shown team coordination to be an important correlate of team performance". In the domain of software development, Nidumolu (1995) shows that higher levels of coordination lead to higher levels of project performance. In their classical work from 1967, Lawrence and Lorsch reported a positive relationship between coordination and organizational performance. Similarly, Simon (1976) states that organizational objectives are achieved through the coordination of the participants' behavior. Finally, Faraj and Xiao (2006, p. 1157) prominently included the positive influence of coordination in their definition by describing coordination as a process to "realize a collective performance".

The outcomes of coordination processes have been characterized in multiple different ways. As previously stated, Okhuysen and Bechky (2009) conceptualize this outcome as coordinated action. Coordination effectiveness by Lee et al. (2013) focuses on the aspects of redundant work and roadblocks in coordination for their construct. Espinosa et al. (2012) introduce the construct coordination problems including items on missed delivery dates, misunderstanding, redundant work etc. This conceptualization is very encompassing concerning coordination problems, but does not depict the underlying forces, which coordination mechanisms seem to influence. Strode et al. (2011) present their conceptualization of coordination effectiveness with the two main dimensions of implicit and explicit coordination outcomes. The implicit domain includes five knowledge related aspects (e.g. know why, know what is going on, know what to do and when, know who is doing what, know who knows what) and three aspects in the explicit dimension (right place, right thing and right time). However, a problem with their view of coordination effectiveness as an outcome construct is the seemingly mediating role the implicit domain plays on the explicit domain. As such, knowing what to do and when, will strongly influence the explicit dimensions *right thing* and *right time*.

To consolidate the widespread knowledge and identify the underlying conditions of coordination, Okhuysen and Bechky (2009) reviewed existing coordination literature in the diverse streams it has been published in and integrated this knowledge back into organizational theory. Previous studies focused on the mechanisms to achieve coordination, their mix within the coordination strategy or the process of coordination to achieve team effectiveness. Therefore, a unified view on the direct conditions, or intermediate states, leading to coordination has remained elusive. Okhuysen and Bechky (2009) propose three integrating conditions that lead to what they refer to as *coordinated action*: (1) *common understanding*, (2) *predictability* and (3) *accountability* (see Table 2.3). Common understanding supports coordinated action "by providing a shared perspective on the whole task and how

Table 2.3 Definitions of integrating conditions for coordinated action

Term	Definition	Source
Common understanding	A shared perspective on the whole task and how individuals' work fits within the whole	Okhuysen and Bechky (2009, p. 488)
Accountability	Addresses the question of who is responsible for specific elements of the task and makes clear where the responsibilities of interdependent parties lie	Okhuysen and Bechky (2009, p. 483)
Predictability	Enables interdependent parties to anticipate subsequent task related activity by knowing what the elements of the task are and when they happen	Okhuysen and Bechky (2009, p. 486)

individuals' work fits within the whole" (Okhuysen and Bechky 2009, p. 488). The aspect of predictability "enables interdependent parties to anticipate subsequent task-related activity by knowing what the elements of the task are and when they happen" (Okhuysen and Bechky 2009, p. 486). Finally, accountability delimits "who is responsible for specific elements of the task" (Okhuysen and Bechky 2009, p. 483). In proposing these three conditions, they stress the importance of the elements that enable coordinated action and "working together and separately, assist in the enactment of coordinated activity" (Okhuysen and Bechky 2009, p. 492). Through the theoretical separation of the coordination mechanism from the coordinated action they support, the intermediate outcomes of these mechanisms can be investigated and explained more deeply (Okhuysen and Bechky 2009).

2.1.5   Summary

The preceding discussion shows the focus areas of the previous literature on coordination. Prior work has concentrated on dependencies between actors in the system to be coordinated and the necessary coordination mechanisms to achieve concerted action, depending on situational factors. This neglects the underlying factors necessary for coordination and posits that one merely needs the correct coordination mechanisms for the situation at hand. Based on Okhuysen and Bechky's (2009) three integrating conditions for coordinated action, common understanding, accountability and predictability, this work tries to fill this gap by empirically investigating inter-team coordination in a field setting.

2.2   Teams and Multiteam Systems

As little is known about the structure of large-scale agile development organizations, a unit of analysis needs to be identified which depicts the organizational structure present in such systems. To benefit from extant knowledge in neighboring disciplines, the multiteam systems unit rooted in organizational psychology is chosen to conceptualize the team of teams setup.

Over the past years, companies have focused more and more on structuring their organization into smaller units of people and thus implementing a team-based organization. "A team [...] can be defined as a collection of individuals who share a common goal, whose actions and outcomes are interdependent, who are perceived by themselves and others as a social entity, and who are embedded in an organizational context" (Devine 2002, p. 291). Previous definitions of software development teams as project teams (Devine 2002; Kozlowski and Bell 2003) see these teams as a temporary unit, assembled for a specific purpose and as soon as their job is done they disband. However, in software product development this is not the case. Here, the team composition is of a permanent nature as the same teams will be developing the next version of the software product they have been working on previously. In this research the team is seen as the smallest entity within a multiteam system consisting of several teams.

With the introduction of agile development approaches in the software industry, the guideline has been to create teams of around seven plus or minus two people and scale this through a hierarchical *team of teams* setup (Larman and Vodde 2008), where several teams have to work closely together in order to release a single software product.

These sorts of collectives have been of ongoing interest to the stream of multiteam systems research. This organizational setup has been defined as a *multiteam system* by Mathieu et al. (2001), who assert that MTSs are "two or more teams that interface directly and interdependently in response to environmental contingencies toward the accomplishment of collective goals" (Mathieu et al. 2001, p. 290). In contrast to other organizational forms such as subsystems (cf. Katz and Kahn 1978) or matrix organizations (cf. Davis and Lawrence 1977), an MTS is a team-based collective with members requiring collaborative integration of teamwork which leads to the high degree of interdependence within MTSs (Zaccaro et al. 2012).

The core elements of an MTS are a goal hierarchy and functional inter-team dependencies. The collective goal of this system can be broken down into a goal hierarchy and constitutes a key characteristic of any MTS. The goal hierarchy marks the boundary of an MTS in that all teams within the system share at least a distal goal while the individual teams pursue their more proximal goals. This structure of goals leads to teams displaying input, process and outcome interdependencies with at least one other team (Mathieu et al. 2001). Within software product development the distal goal of all involved teams is the completion of a new release of the software that is being implemented. The proximal goals of each team within the MTS usually comprise of responsibility for a software subcomponent of the product or of certain features to be added to the next release of the software.

Over the past decades, research on teams has been widespread, leading to a deep understanding of team processes and work (cf. Guzzo and Dickson 1996; Ilgen et al. 2004; Kozlowski and Bell 2003; Mathieu and Maynard 2008). Our understanding of multiteam systems and especially these systems in a software development environment remains exceptionally limited.

2.3 Agile Software Development

The history of agile software development is often traced back to the Agile Manifesto in the year 2001 (Fowler and Highsmith 2001). The origins of the underlying concepts, namely iterative and incremental development, reach as far back as the 1950s (Larman and Basili 2003). Even early plan-based approaches established iterative feedback as an essential element. The waterfall model (Benington 1956), often described as the foe of serious agilists, showed first beginnings of iterative ideas through Royce's (1970) adaptation, which included iterative feedback.

Over the years, newer software development models have continued to include more and more ideas based on iterations and feedback. Starting with the spiral model, the notion of several iterations was codified into the development process as a core component (Boehm 1988). While the waterfall model is heavily specification driven, the spiral model is driven by risk management. In the 1990s, resulting from the proliferation of object-oriented programming languages and design, the Rational Unified Process (RUP) (Kruchten 1998) was specified to be model- or architecture-based. It distinguished itself by constituting a process framework, which can be adapted to the setting in which it is deployed.

What all of these process models have in common is their rather heavyweight approach to process management, specifications and large design upfront based on documents, and comparatively long iteration cycles. As a countermovement to these heavyweight models, the mid-1990s saw a push towards more lightweight processes.

One of the first was the Dynamic Systems Development Method (DSDM Consortium, n.d.) in 1994. It values eight principles: (1) Focus on the business need, (2) deliver on time, (3) collaborate, (4) never compromise quality, (5) build incrementally from firm foundations, (6) develop iteratively, (7) communicate continuously and clearly and (8) demonstrate control. A year later, Scrum was first publicly presented (Sutherland and Schwaber 1995). It defines a project management framework based on time-boxed iterations with defined roles and a focus on face-to-face communication. Extreme Programming (XP) saw the light of day in 1996 and was later published in book form (Beck 2001). It is based on a set of values, fundamental principles, activities and practices. In contrast to Scrum, XP defines technical practices for the development work of programmers.

In 2001, several prominent advocates of lightweight development methods gathered to create the Agile Manifesto (Fowler and Highsmith 2001). They proposed four values, which constitute the essence of agile development methods:

individuals and interactions over processes and tool

working software over comprehensive documentation

customer collaboration over contract negotiation

responding to change over following a plan

The first value emphasizes the people orientation of the agile movement. The relationships between team members, customers and partners are valued above prescribed processes and some methods' heavy reliance on cumbersome tools. Agile methods value close proximity in the form of co-location and intensive team communication. In the end, a piece of working software is more useful than a sizeable documentation of software that is not what the customer wanted or even worse, unusable. At the end of short iterations, the goal is to present an increment of working software to the customer for validation. With the help of automated testing, quality, as part of the 'working' software, is ensured. Trust between customer and development team is the essential foundation of agile methods. Instead of stressing precise contracts, the customer is involved very heavily in the development of the software to ensure he is satisfied with the product. As agile focuses on fast value delivery, risk is minimized for the customer as well. The last value points to the core of agile development, the necessity to adapt to a changing environment. All people involved in an agile project, the customers and the developers, both experts in their field, can judge if a project needs to adjust to better satisfy the needs of the customer and not just plainly follow a specified plan.

These values illustrate the considerable mind shift in agile software development, which emphasizes cross-functional teams with time-boxed development phases and continuous management of requirements. Abrahamsson et al. (2002) state that a development method is agile when it is incremental, cooperative, straightforward and adaptive. This differs strongly from traditional development. The core differences between agile development and traditional approaches are summarized by Nerur et al. (2005) in Table 2.4.

Table 2.4 Traditional versus agile software development

	Traditional development	Agile development
Fundamental assumptions	Systems are fully specifiable, predictable, and are built through meticulous and extensive planning	High-quality software is developed by small teams using the principles of continuous design improvement and testing based on rapid feedback and change
Control	Process centric	People centric
Management style	Command and control	Leadership and collaboration
Knowledge management	Explicit	Tacit
Role assignment	Individual—favors specialization	Self-organizing teams—encourages role inter-changeability
Communication	Formal	Informal
Customer's role	Important	Critical
Development model	Life-cycle model (waterfall, spiral or some variation)	The evolutionary-delivery model
Desired organizational form	Mechanistic (bureaucratic with high formalization), aimed at large organizations	Organic (flexible and participative encouraging cooperative social action), aimed at small and medium-sized organizations

Based on Nerur et al. (2005, p. 75)

While many methods are considered agile, only a select few have become prominent in industry. By far the most widely used method is Scrum (VersionOne Inc. 2013). The following section will give an overview of the Scrum framework.

2.3.1 The Scrum Framework

Originally presented at a conference in 1995 (Sutherland and Schwaber 1995), the idea is based on research from Takeuchi and Nonaka (1986) who investigated new product development in Japan and the United States. The investigated companies have taken a new approach to product development, which they named the rugby approach. Companies utilizing this approach show six characteristics of new product development: (1) built-in instability, (2) self-organizing project teams, (3) overlapping development phases, (4) multilearning, (5) subtle control and (6) organizational transfer of learning (Takeuchi and Nonaka 1986).

Built-in instability is created by top management, which tasks a project team with a very challenging goal and gives the team great freedom in achieving this goal. Because of this freedom, the project team can act like a start-up company in taking initiatives and risks. Instead of relying on a sequential order of process phases, these phases overlap to minimize bottlenecks that may lead to a system standstill. Through overlapping project phases, shared responsibility and commitment are increased. For example, the involvement of production experts in early phases can accelerate the development process, as feedback concerning the production is gathered early on and not in one of the later phases. Multilearning involves gathering information from outside in order to respond quickly to a changing market. On the team level, continuous learning is necessary, as the challenging goals need new strategies to solve them. In contrast to the command and control style of management, the rugby approach suggests self-control and control through peer pressure as ways to manage such projects. Starting with the right people in an open work environment, tolerating mistakes and rewarding group performance as opposed to individual performance, leads to more subtle ways of management being able to control such projects. An organizational transfer of learning is achieved by assigning key people to follow-up projects to promote what they have previously learned (Takeuchi and Nonaka 1986).

Based on the presented rugby approach to new product development, the Scrum framework was established for software development projects. While often referred to as a software development method, Scrum is strictly speaking a project management framework for software development projects. Within this framework, no technical aspects of development work are defined. What follows is an in-depth look at the Scrum framework based on its roles, events and artifacts (based on Deemer et al. 2012; Schwaber and Beedle 2002; Schwaber and Sutherland 2013).

The *Product Owner* (PO) is responsible for the business value of the product to be developed. He identifies product features and translates these into an ordered list, with the highest value items on top. This role has the sole responsibility for the profit or loss of the developed product. In general, there are two scenarios for the role of the Product Owner. In the first case, the customer and the Product Owner is the same person, which is often the case in internal development projects. The other option is the Product Owner as the representative of the customer, of whom there might be many in the market. In this case, he consolidates the customers' needs and requirements to form a backlog (Deemer et al. 2012).

The *development team* implements the backlog items specified by the Product Owner. There should be no fixed specialists, such as tester or architect, only team members. The team is cross-functional and includes all necessary expertise to implement the backlog items and deliver a potentially shippable product at the end of a sprint. Areas of expertise that do not yet exist within the team are expected to be acquired through continuous learning. As a self-organizing and autonomous team, the members decide which set of backlog items to implement from those specified and prioritized by the Product Owner. The team is most effective if all members of the team are allocated one hundred percent to one product and do not switch between projects, which avoids costly context switching. The size of a development team is specified to be seven plus minus two people. Ideally, a Scrum team is co-located (Deemer et al. 2012).

The *Scrum Master* (SM) acts as a facilitator to the development team and the Product Owner. He helps both to learn and apply the Scrum process and is an essential figure in Scrum's fundamental principle 'inspect and adapt'. Contrary to other project management approaches, the Scrum Master is not a project manager as he neither manages the team, nor manages the product under development. In some team setups, he also takes on part-time development duties. The Scrum Master does not have people management responsibilities; instead, he acts as a coach and teacher and ensures that the Scrum process is followed. Furthermore, he makes sure that impediments are taken care of and resolved. As Scrum usually entails a cultural change within the organization, the Scrum Master guides not only the team and the Product Owner through this change, but also helps the larger organization in implementing Scrum (Deemer et al. 2012).

At the center of Scrum lies the *sprint*, a time-boxed period during which a potentially shippable software product increment is built. In practice, the sprint is usually two or four weeks long. During a development effort, one sprint follows the next to form a continuous succession. Within one sprint, no changes are allowed in the product backlog that would jeopardize the current sprint goal as agreed upon between team and Product Owner. If backlog items turn out to be larger or more difficult than initially expected, items can be de-committed and moved to the next sprint in order to still successfully complete the other items (Schwaber and Sutherland 2013).

As the name suggests, the *sprint planning* is a meeting to prepare for the upcoming sprint. It should answer what will be delivered and how this will be done. In the first part of this meeting, the Product Owner and the team examine what has been determined as the sprint goal. Continuing, the backlog items necessary to achieve that goal are examined and discussed to establish a common understanding of the functionality to be developed. Based on the value-ordered list of backlog items in the product backlog, the team chooses which items to pick for the next sprint. This selection is usually based on the team's capacity in the upcoming sprint and their past performance. The second part of the planning meeting pertains to how the items in the sprint backlog will be implemented. The team starts by designing the work needed to transform the selected backlog items into a working product increment. At the end of the sprint planning meeting it should be clear what the team commits itself to implement and how this will be done (Schwaber and Sutherland 2013).

The *daily Scrum* is a 15-min meeting recurring every day. It is often called *daily standup*, to show that it is intended to be a quick meeting. In this time-boxed event, the development team synchronizes its activities and creates a plan for the next 24 h. During the meeting, each team member answers three questions: (1) 'What did I accomplish yesterday?', (2) 'What will I do before the next daily Scrum meeting?' and (3) 'Are there obstacles in the way?'. The developers give answers to these questions to the other team members. The daily Scrum is not intended to be a status meeting towards the Scrum Master or other roles, it is purely from the team for the team. The Scrum Master is responsible for removing impediments that were brought up in the daily Scrum. No in-depth discussion is supposed to take place in this daily meeting. If further clarification is needed this can be scheduled for interested parties directly after the daily Scrum meeting (Schwaber and Sutherland 2013).

The product backlog refinement is an ongoing process, usually done in the form of a workshop. No more than ten percent of the team's capacity for the sprint should be spent on this activity. This activity, also called *backlog grooming*, is meant to split large backlog items, estimate and prioritize them for future sprints. Both the Product Owner and the development team attend this activity. If this refinement is done regularly, the sprint planning meeting should become relatively simple as the items on the top of the backlog will be prepared in detail, meaning their content and business value is clear as well as an effort estimate available (Deemer et al. 2012).

The *sprint review* is a meeting where all involved stakeholders review the work done during the sprint. Based on the principle of 'inspect and adapt', this meeting focuses on the product. It should allow for an in-depth conversation on specific details of the product, giving the Product Owner the chance to see what is going on within the team and the software and giving the team the chance to learn from the Product Owner what is going on in the market. The team presents the latest software product increment in a live demo. Thereby, all people present have the chance to interact and inspect the software and give feedback to the team (Deemer et al. 2012).

In the *sprint retrospective*, the focus is on team-internal processes and their environment. Here, the team discusses what works well and what does not. At the end of the retrospective, major items that went well and improvement areas are identified. Moreover, a plan for implementing actions regarding these areas is agreed upon (Schwaber and Sutherland 2013).

The *product backlog* is a list of customer-focused items that are desired in the product. The individual backlog items are ordered according to the Product

Owner's perception of their business value. The product backlog is a living artifact as it never stops changing. The Product Owner refines backlog items, changes their value and the team estimates the effort needed to implement the items. The higher an item is ranked in the backlog the more detailed and refined it has become. Items further down on the list are more granular and less detailed (Schwaber and Sutherland 2013).

A *product increment* is the sum of the work completed in the current sprint and all previous ones. It is a potentially shippable product state and must be in a usable condition. The *definition of done* is a shared understanding of when a backlog item is done. This definition can include minimum requirements concerning the documentation or functionality tests for the developed increment. The Product Owner and the team need to agree on this definition and it should continually evolve with the maturity of the team (Schwaber and Sutherland 2013).

2.3.2   Agile Software Development on the Team Level

As agile software development originated from small-scale settings, much of the research has focused on the team level. Here, the effects of individual agile techniques such as pair programming or test-driven development (Balijepally et al. 2009; Erdogmus et al. 2005; Mangalaraj et al. 2009) were a natural point of departure for research.

In a literature review by Erickson et al. (2005), research in the fields of Agile Methodology, Agile Modelling and Extreme Programming with a focus on the later was found. Within the XP publications, two main directions are visible. On the one hand, there are case studies with experience reports of practitioners, which cover the XP approach as a whole, and on the other, there is research on individual or small sets of the core XP practices. The mentioned case studies are lacking detail and generally conclude with the positive assessment of XP as a development method. As an individual practice, mostly pair programming was studied, providing mixed results. Erickson et al. conclude with "hard, empirically-based economic evidence is lacking" and "other empirical efforts to study XP, in total or its core practices, are quite limited as well" (Erickson et al. 2005).

Subsequently, a broader avenue of inquiry was followed concentrating on four main categories: introduction and adoption, human and social factors, customer and developer perceptions and comparative studies (Dybå and Dingsøyr 2008). Dybå and Dingsøyr (2008) report a total of 1996 studies published until 2005 with only 36 showing acceptable rigor, credibility and relevance, most dealing with XP. Within the four identified categories following research was observed.

Introduction and adoption. Although easy to adopt and introduce in small organizations, agile processes can prove to be difficult to implement in complex organizations. Especially practices that involve testing (test-first or continuous testing) need to be introduced early as it takes time and effort to properly embrace these concepts. Nevertheless, test-first programming contributed to higher quality in code as did pair programming, which, in addition, also enhanced learning among team members. However, a few developers mention it to be exhausting, inefficient and a waste of time, suggesting an attitude polarization among users of that practice. It was found that XP worked best with experienced programmers who have a solid domain knowledge. On the management side, training has to occur simultaneously as technical problems appear earlier, which can lead to unfamiliar situations with issues being raised too early for management. Overall, XP teams showed that improved communication with continuous feedback seems to be a key success factor, although many XP teams were perceived as being more isolated by other teams.

Human and social factors. Evidence of agile teams having faith in their own abilities, while showing respect and responsibility, has surfaced. Moreover, trust is pervasive and goes beyond pair-partner trust, as it was also found to be true across pairs and sub teams. The skills of good XP team members are described as analytical, good people-skills and an affinity for learning.

Customer and developer perceptions. Customers appreciated the agile development process, as daily meetings kept them up to date and the higher involvement reduced confusion about development questions. However, this high customer involvement seems to be unsustainable as planning, testing and retrospective activities are demanding and require the customer to acclimatize to each development organization. The developers' perception of XP and Scrum is very good with employees claiming that pair programming sped up the development process and Scrum led to a reduction of overtime.

Comparative studies. In comparison to a more traditional incremental approach, the agile approach allowed the incorporation of changes at later stages with less impact on the overall project. Furthermore, the presentation of working software to the customer combined with his continuous feedback led to a sharp increase in customer satisfaction and an earlier demonstration of business value. In four studies comparing traditional development methods with XP, the productivity differences vary extremely and do not allow for drawing sensible conclusions. This may in part be due to the inherent difficulty of measuring software development productivity and as Dybå and Dingsøyr (2008) mention, the studies did not have an appropriate recruitment strategy to ensure unbiased comparisons. However, many developers themselves indicated that their productivity increased with the introduction of XP. The aspect of product quality can also be characterized as varying, although the quality differences are in a much narrower interval in comparison to productivity. Over all, the improvement of quality ranges from no difference to a 65% improvement in prerelease quality. In a study comparing developers using XP practices with ones that did not, the XP users were more satisfied and comfortable with their jobs (Dybå and Dingsøyr 2008). The studies show a clear bias towards XP and relatively young development teams. They conclude with the finding that both the number and the quality of studies on agile software development needed to be increased (Dybå and Dingsøyr 2008).

Diverging from co-located small-scale settings, Jalali and Wohlin (2012) focused on research on agile practices in distributed settings, in which globally distributed teams collaborated over a long time on small to medium-sized projects. They agree that the majority of existing literature is in the form of industrial experience reports. The most common practices found were continuous integration, daily standup meetings, pair programming, retrospectives, Scrum of Scrums meetings and test-driven development. Furthermore, many agile practices had been customized to fit their environment (Jalali and Wohlin 2012). They conclude that an insufficient number of studies analyzing the challenges of applying agile in distributed settings has been conducted in order to conclude that agile was efficiently applicable in large distributed projects. The authors demand for further research on modifications of agile methods to support practitioners with guidelines on how to adapt practices to their needs (Jalali and Wohlin 2012).

Recently, Chuang et al. (2014) published a bibliometric analysis of agile literature in the years between 2001 and 2012. Key outlets for agile research, top individual contributors, most cited articles as well as institutions and countries most engaged in agile research were identified. They conclude with the need for more research not only of a practical but of a scholarly nature in particular, since most research on agile development methods are at the infancy stage (Chuang et al. 2014).

The preceding discussion shows that in the domain of agile software development much of the recent literature has focused on individual practices and adoption of agile methods. After having presented the current state of research on agile software development on the team level, the following chapter delves into the topic of large-scale agile development.

2.3.3   Industrial Frameworks for Large-Scale Agile Development

The foundations of large-scale agile development lie in the previously presented agile development approaches. These are extended or modified to better support the differing large-scale environment. Before presenting the practical approaches to scaling agile development, a fundamental question needs to be answered: How big is large-scale?

This question remains unresolved although a few attempts have been made to come to a consistent definition. Participants of the workshop 'Towards Principles of Large-Scale Agile Development' as part of the XP2014 conference (Dingsøyr and Moe 2014) have gathered definitions of large-scale agile development, which can be seen in Table 2.5. Work done by Dingsøyr et al. (2014) suggest that a taxonomy of scale in agile development should best be based on the number of teams involved in the development project. They suggest three levels: (1) small-scale (one team), (2) large-scale (two to nine teams) and (3) very large-scale (ten teams or more).

When transferring agile into large settings, the differences become very obvious. As soon as several teams have to cooperate to develop one piece of software, the coordination overhead becomes elevated as now communication and coordination

Table 2.5 Definitions of large-scale agile development

Over 50 developers OR 1/2 million lines of code OR more than 3 sites/time zones
Over 50 persons, over 5 teams, developing together the same product/project using agile method
Agile being applied to more than one team, one project, one product
Multiple teams working together in order to deliver software artefacts

Based on Dingsøyr and Moe (2014)

lines increase many times over. Not only the number of people involved adds complexity, in large organizations with many locations, the distributed nature of such development setups brings challenges in the form of temporal, geographic and socio-cultural differences (Hossain et al. 2009). Furthermore, many large development efforts are of a product development nature, i.e. the continuous development of one product over many years. This leads to a considerable code history, or legacy code, that needs to be dealt with. To overcome these challenges and give guidance to practitioners, several frameworks have been developed to scale agile methods to large settings. The frameworks, Large-Scale Scrum (LeSS) (Larman and Vodde, n.d.), Scaled Agile Framework (SAFe) (Leffingwell, n.d.) and Scaled Professional Scrum (Nexus) (Schwaber et al., n.d.) will be presented in the following sections.

Large-Scale Scrum. This is an approach that sets out to scale Scrum within the constraints of pure Scrum. Essentially, LeSS is regular Scrum applied to large-scale settings. While it attempts to preserve the strengths of Scrum, it reinforces the need for more process clarity with defined structures. Within the LeSS framework, two variants exist, one for two to eight teams and one for more than eight teams (Larman and Vodde, n.d.).

Variant A keeps all the basic roles of Scrum unchanged but adapts the meeting structure. The previously mentioned sprint planning meeting is held with representatives of each team, so as not to gather too many people in one meeting. At the end of the sprint, a cross-team retrospective is added to advance the overall system improvement. To support inter-team coordination, additional meetings such as Scrum of Scrums can be added. Scrum of Scrums is a meeting to synchronize inter-team activities. Representatives of each team gather regularly, similar to the daily Scrum, to discuss ongoing implementations and current impediments (Larman and Vodde, n.d.).

Variant B, for systems with more than eight teams, introduces the additional role of an Area Product Owner (APO). This role is responsible for requirement areas, which are customer-centric clusters of product backlog items. The leading Product Owner groups each product backlog item into one requirement area and hands the responsibility to the corresponding Area Product Owner. This item is then prioritized by the Area Product Owner who specializes in one part of the product from the customer perspective. Each requirement area has several teams working in it that pull their items from the area backlog. A requirement area is organized around customer centric requirements, while traditional development areas are organized around the product architecture (Larman and Vodde, n.d.).

Scaled Agile Framework. This framework operates on three levels, portfolio, program and team (Leffingwell, n.d.). Within the portfolio area, individuals are responsible for strategic themes, investment budgets and their allocation to release trains. These release trains essentially constitute individual programs or products in development. The high-level portfolio backlog is broken down into the program backlogs, which are then broken down into the team backlogs. The program level management takes the program epics (high-level backlog items) from the portfolio level and creates a vision and a product roadmap, which guide the development in the next releases. A product increment starts with a planning event, where the program management introduces the vision for the upcoming release and each team plans their individual share of the total development effort. The team level is made up of the cross-functional development teams, which pick their backlog items from the team backlogs (Leffingwell, n.d.).

Scaled Professional Scrum. The Scaled Professional Scrum framework (Nexus) was created by some of the initial developers of Scrum and considers the inter-operation of teams and dependencies between them, the main challenge of scaling Scrum. This framework introduces a team called the 'nexus' integration team that is responsible for successful integration of the work done by the individual development teams. A nexus consists of no more than nine teams, which need to integrate their work in order to create a potentially shippable product increment (Schwaber et al., n.d.).

All three frameworks try to scale agile development to multiple teams, however, the direction of their approaches seems very different. While Large-Scale Scrum and Scaled Professional Scrum are at their hearts Scrum scaled to several teams with only slight modifications, the Scaled Agile Framework is much more heavyweight and encompassing. LeSS and Nexus clearly come from the agile side and try to transfer the basic values and concepts to large-scale settings, while SAFe approaches from the more heavyweight side of the spectrum and tries to bring in agile. On the one hand, the lacking involvement of higher management in the LeSS and Nexus approach is covered explicitly in SAFe, but on the other hand, LeSS and Nexus seem much closer to the original principles of the agile development movement.

Furthermore, one could question the applicability of such industrial scale frameworks, as they mostly tend to assume a green field approach. However, taking into account the previously mentioned environmental factors of large organizations that gradually adopt more lightweight development methods, such radical frameworks that require not only a change of the organizational culture, but also an entire restructuring of the development workforce, might not always be applicable in practice. Oftentimes, adapted or contextualized (cf. Hoda et al. 2010) forms of large-scale agile development approaches are more realistic to be implemented. They do not pose those kind of risks to the organization that often come along with a major restructuring.

2.3.4 Agile Software Development on the Multiteam System Level

Since the origins of agile development lie in small team contexts, the associated methods have only recently and hesitantly been promoted and studied in large-scale settings. Only 23 papers could be identified, which deal with large-scale agile software development. All papers were reviewed for their coverage of large-scale agile and classified according to their research method, approach and general topic area. The following paragraphs will present the found literature, structured according to type.

The largest group of literature belonged to the *experience reports*. Within this group, several papers illustrate how agile was implemented and what pitfalls were discovered. Many also described the way these impediments were solved within the context of the implementing organization (Benefield 2008; Fry and Greene 2007; Lee 2008; Moore and Spens 2008; Paasivaara and Lassenius 2011; Smits and Pshigoda 2007; Sutherland et al. 2009). Paasivaara et al. (2014) report on the introduction of so called 'Value Workshops' to come to a common understanding across the teams about which values the development area has and how to promote them. Three models of architecture support are proposed by Eckstein (2014) to promote emergent architecture within large-scale agile development systems.

Articles in the group of *conceptual literature* try to shed light on fundamental questions within large-scale agile development. As such, Dingsøyr et al. (2014) examine the concept of size based on the number of teams in one development system. They come to the definition that two to nine teams are to be considered large-scale, while ten and more teams should be considered very large-scale. Twenty-one principles of scaled agile are proposed in Laanti (2014) including the notion of controlling processes as opposed to people or to utilize tacit knowledge. Kettunen and Laanti (2008) introduce a framework for understanding the multi-dimensional nature of agility within large organizations. Finally, Power (2014) develops a decision support model for distinguishing what the 'large' is referring to in pursuing agile in an organization. He distinguishes between three different large settings: the implementation in one team in a large organization, the use of agile across a large project or if organizational agility is strived for.

The final group consists of two *empirical articles*, which investigate networking and productivity respectively. Moe et al. (2014) investigated through a case study how a newly introduced role of technical area responsible supports knowledge networks between teams. They conclude that this role is central in the knowledge network and acts as a boundary spanner between teams. Furthermore, the size of the knowledge network depended heavily on the company tenure of the team members. Productivity and delays are the core topics in a study by Badampudi et al. (2013). Through a Grounded Theory interview study of five projects, the challenges within those projects were identified. It was revealed that the influencing factors within requirements creation and use, namely collaboration and knowledge management, were predominantly influencing productivity and delays.

2.4   Prior Work on Coordination in Multiteam Systems and Large-Scale Agile Development

Although a considerable amount of research on agile software development has been published (see Sects. 2.3.2 and 2.3.4), the specific topic of coordination in agile multiteam systems remains neglected in previous literature. The following sections present the scarce extant work on coordination in multiteam systems and coordination in large-scale agile development.

2.4.1   Coordination in Multiteam Systems

While the concept of MTS has received increasing attention in organizational psychology over the last decade (e.g. Asencio et al. 2012; Davison et al. 2012; DeChurch and Marks 2006; Lanaj et al. 2012), the topic of coordination is underdeveloped within this stream as well. Marks et al. (2001) present a time-based conceptual framework of team processes, including action and transition episodes. Action phases primarily include activities directly related to goal accomplishment, and transition phases include evaluation or planning activities. Within MTSs, the management of these performance episodes is viewed as a central part of coordination (DeChurch and Marks 2006). Marks et al. (2005) found that cross-team processes had the most value in MTSs with a highly interdependent goal hierarchy. Well-managed MTS transition processes influenced MTS performance positively, but did not support team level action processes. Decentralized planning led to enhanced multiteam system performance by fostering proactivity and higher aspiration levels. Nevertheless, strong negative effects were found in excessive risk seeking and coordination failures (Lanaj et al. 2012).

Asencio et al. (2012) propose multiteam charters as a means to develop efficient leadership structures and communication networks. Boundary spanners and communication norms across teams are mentioned as important considerations in MTS collaboration. These differentiated team roles are viewed as a key factor for performance by Davison et al. (2012). Teams that included boundary spanning roles consistently outperformed teams that did not. The reasoning lies in the information processing complexity inherent in large organizations, which leads to the need for formalized boundary spanning (Davison et al. 2012).

In their study of leadership in multiteam systems, DeChurch and Marks (2006) trained teams of leaders in two ways, either by facilitating strategy development or coordination. They found that strategy training was positively related to explicit coordination, with coordination training affecting implicit coordination more heavily.

Beyond these first forays, little is known about coordination in MTSs. However, the notion of cross-team processes (Marks et al. 2005) including communication across teams (Asencio et al. 2012) suggests the importance of directionality of coordination in MTSs. Furthermore, the aspect of decentralized planning (Lanaj et al. 2012) conveys the influence of coordination locality in MTSs.

2.4.2 Coordination in Large-Scale Agile Development

The topic of coordination in large-scale agile development literature is extremely scarce. Overall, only six papers were identified that approach the topic of coordination in large-scale settings. The following sections present these articles according to the areas they focus on.

Challenges of Coordination through Representatives. Paasivaara et al. (2012) report on a case study of two distributed large-scale Scrum projects. Both projects comprised of at least twenty teams and were distributed worldwide. The practice under study was the Scrum of Scrums meeting, whereby representatives of each team meet regularly to discuss current issues and future topics on an inter-team level. The results show that, with the amount of teams present in each project, the individual interests of all participants were too wide to be of interest to everybody else. Furthermore, some representatives did not know what to report and so did not contribute anything to the meeting. A possible solution that was implemented was a feature-specific Scrum of Scrums meeting for the teams working together on one feature. A location specific Scrum of Scrums meeting was reported as not working very well. Similarly, Hole and Moe (2008) found that modularization of the software enables agility and supports Scrum of Scrums meetings. However, they report that co-location was a facilitator of this type of meeting.

Influences on Coordination Mechanisms and Coordination Strategies. Hole and Moe (2008) investigated how three distributed projects applying agile methods coordinated their work. They observed that in order to reduce standardization and direct supervision in global software development projects, trust was an essential trait. Furthermore, the possibility for short exchanges via online messengers supported mutual adjustment. Li and Maedche (2012) present preliminary results of a study to show what factors influence the formation of coordination strategies. In an agile distributed software development setting, a difference in time zones seemed to increase the use of mechanistic coordination. Both mechanistic and organic coordination mechanisms were needed to cope with changing customer requirements. Finally, the introduction of explicit coordination mechanisms improved mutual trust and shared cognition of long-standing colleagues through intensified communication and agile practices (Li and Maedche 2012). Scheerer et al. (2014) present different conceptual coordination strategy types for inter-team coordination. These types are based on the amount of existing mechanistic, organic and cognitive coordination and are illustrated with examples from large-scale agile product development settings.

Challenges and Their Alleviation in Large-Scale Agile Development. Lagerberg et al. (2013) present results of a quantitative study on two projects with 14 and 15 teams respectively. Only one of the two projects had fully implemented agile development methods. From the comparison between the two, agile methods facilitated knowledge sharing and increased visibility of the status of other teams. Based on the higher awareness of other teams in the agile project, they concluded that a higher inter-team and intra-team coordination effectiveness was present in comparison to the non-agile project. Lagerberg et al. (2013) propose that the use of complete teams with feature responsibility and open space offices contributed to the higher coordination effectiveness. Scheerer et al. (2015) describe the problem of sequential task dependencies in agile backlogs within multiteam development settings. Through a simulative modeling approach, they conclude that the degree of freedom a Product Owner has in choosing a backlog order is severely limited. As such, one dependency already limits his choice by 50%. In order to mitigate this problem they suggest dependency avoidance through different team structures within multiteam systems or the early detection and active management of dependencies through techniques such as user story mapping or dedicated dependency tracking practices.

Overall, the previous literature remains very limited. However, Hole and Moe's (2008) study suggests that different locations influence the chosen coordination types while Paasivaara et al. (2012) findings advocate an influence of development system size on the direction of coordination. Finally, work done by Scheerer et al. (2015) shows the influence of task dependencies on the coordination of software development MTSs. After having illustrated the limited previous work on coordination in MTSs and large-scale agile development, what follows next is the construction of the research framework underlying this study.

2.5   Research Framework

The point of departure for this study is the view that coordinated action is a necessary condition for organizational performance (cf. Cheng 1984; Lawrence and Lorsch 1967; Simon 1976). Therefore, the perspective of Okhuysen and Bechky (2009) and Kotlarsky et al. (2008) is taken that coordination is an outcome state in the form of coordinated action which in turn necessitates the integrating conditions common understanding, predictability and accountability (see Sect. 2.1.4).

Coordination Configuration. The notion of a coordination strategy is expanded upon by the introduction of a *coordination configuration*. While previous research has examined types of coordination mechanisms (cf. Strode et al. 2012) and their direction in conjunction with their location (cf. Nidumolu 1995, 1996), to the best of the author's knowledge no study has incorporated all three aspects of coordination type, locus, and direction into one configuration. The coordination configuration is based on the previously discussed literature (see Sect. 2.1) with three core dimensions. The *coordination type* describes the type of coordination mechanisms in use and ranges from a pure mechanistic approach to a predominantly organic type (Espinosa et al. 2010; Thompson 1967; Van De Ven et al. 1976). The *coordination locus* resembles what Mintzberg (1980) calls decentralization of decision making (see Sect. 2.1.1) in that it signifies the location in the multiteam system where coordination activities take place. It ranges from a primarily centralized system, e.g. with decisions about coordination situated centrally in the MTS, to a decentralized approach, e.g. where coordination is located in a more dispersed fashion among the individual teams within the MTS. Within the *coordination direction* dimension, the orientation of communication necessary for coordination is depicted. This can occur either in a vertical fashion across hierarchical levels or within one level between different actors of the latter (Davison et al. 2012; Mintzberg 1980; Nidumolu 1995; Van De Ven et al. 1976). The three dimensions can be arranged to form archetypes, of which two are outlined in Fig. 2.1. *Top-down planning* represents a mechanistic, centralized approach with predominantly vertical coordination. On the other hand, *bottom-up adjustment* is portrayed as a largely organic and decentralized strategy with horizontal coordination. These two extreme ends of a continuum do not represent a general, static orientation towards coordination in a multiteam system. Rather, these archetypes together with multiple variations in between, are to be understood as a set of coordination configurations that together form a change process in reaction to a discrete event. The integrating conditions for coordination are established by enacting specific coordination configurations that are a composite of the just mentioned dimensions within the configuration.

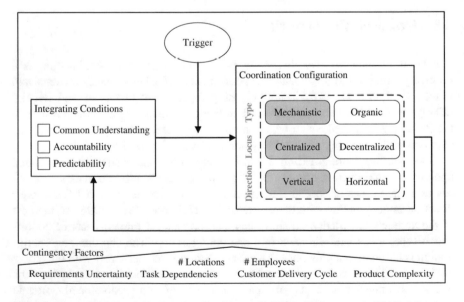

Fig. 2.1 Research Framework. Based on Davison et al. (2012), Espinosa et al. (2010), Mintzberg (1980), Okhuysen and Bechky (2009), Thompson (1967), Van De Ven et al. (1976)

Trigger. Other studies have viewed the link between coordination mechanisms and the situational context in terms of fit. That is, the utilized coordination mechanisms are based on situational factors of the coordination process, i.e. time zone differences require more mechanistic coordination or higher project complexity increases the frequency of synchronization activities (cf. Li and Maedche 2012; Strode et al. 2012). This study views the enacted coordination configuration as a reaction to a trigger within the multiteam system. Therefore, the previously static view of the coordination strategy is altered into a quasi-dynamic one, as this research proposes a time-dependent view of the coordination process. These triggers can manifest in different ways. Poole et al. (2000) characterize two causal forces, ones that operate continuously and others that only come into play at specific points in time. The more apparent trigger is what will be called the discrete exogenous trigger. These types of trigger are of a discrete nature and can be attributed to a specific point in time. The second type is what will be called a latent endogenous trigger. These are more slowly moving causes which are of a latent nature and build up over time until a threshold is reached whence they act to trigger a change (Grzymala-Busse 2010).

Integrating Conditions. Previous studies (see Sect. 2.1) have considered the direct influence of coordination mechanisms, e.g. coordination by plan or rules, or coordination by mutual adjustment, on coordination outcomes. As the underlying factors that coordination, especially task coordination, tries to achieve are not considered, the conditions as proposed by Okhuysen and Bechky (2009) are viewed as the integrating conditions to be achieved for coordinated action to occur (see Sect. 2.1.4). As the focus of this study lies on task coordination and not on execution activities, coordinated action can be regarded as the outcome of the integrating conditions common understanding, predictability and accountability, while the task coordination activities are depicted through the coordination configuration.

Contingency Factors. The coordination within an MTS and thus the enacted coordination configuration may be influenced by contingent factors, which impel the system to react in different ways based on the manifestation of these factors. Organizational aspects such as the number of locations (Hole and Moe 2008) and employees (Paasivaara et al. 2012) of an MTS may influence coordination. Furthermore, procedural traits in the form of customer delivery cycles affect the time available to coordinate tasks and thus may affect coordination. Finally, aspects such as requirements uncertainty, product complexity (Tatikonda and Rosenthal 2000) and task dependencies (Scheerer et al. 2015) have been shown to have an impact on planning and task coordination procedures within MTSs and thus lead to an altered coordination configuration enactment.

In conclusion, the preliminary research framework acts as a frame to examine and illustrate changes in the coordination configuration originating from a triggering event. These changes lead to the establishment of integrating conditions that are viewed as preconditions for coordinated action.

References

Abrahamsson, P., Salo, O., Ronkainen, J., & Warsta, J. (2002). Agile software development methods. *Vtt Publications, 478*(3), 167–168. Retrieved from http://citeseerx.ist.psu.edu/viewdoc/download?doi=10.1.1.161.5931&rep=rep1&type=pdf

Asencio, R., Carter, D. R., DeChurch, L. A., Zaccaro, S. J., & Fiore, S. M. (2012). Charting a course for collaboration: A multiteam perspective. *Translational Behavioral Medicine, 2*(4), 487–494. Retrieved from http://link.springer.com/article/10.1007/s13142-012-0170-3

Bacharach, S. B. (1989). Organizational theories: Some criteria for evaluation. *Academy of Management Review, 14*(4), 496–515.

Badampudi, D., Fricker, B., & Moreno, A. M. (2013). Perspectives on productivity and delays in large-scale agile projects. In *Proceedings of the 14th International Conference Agile Processes in Software Engineering and Extreme Programming* (pp. 180–194).

Balijepally, V., Mahapatra, R., Nerur, S. P., & Price, K. H. (2009). Are two heads better than one for software development? The productivity paradox of pair programming. *MIS Quarterly, 33* (1), 91–118. Retrieved from http://aisel.aisnet.org/misq/vol33/iss1/7/

Beck, K. (2001). *Extreme programming explained: Embrace change.* Addison-Wesley Professional.

Benefield, G. (2008). Rolling out agile in a large enterprise. In *Proceedings of the Annual Hawaii International Conference on System Sciences* (pp. 1–10).

Benington, H. D. (1956). Production of large computer programs. In *Proceedings, ONR Symposium on Advanced Programming Methods for Digital Computers, June 1956* (pp. 15–27).

Boehm, B. (1988). A spiral model of software development and enhancement. *Computer, 21*(5), 61–72.

Cannon-Bowers, J. A., Salas, E., & Converse, S. (1993). Shared mental models in expert team decision making. In N. John Castellan (Ed.), *Current issues in individual and group decision making* (pp. 221–246).

Cheng, J. L. C. (1984). Organizational coordination, uncertainty, and performance: An integrative study. *Human Relations, 37*(10), 829–851.

Chuang, S.-W., Luor, T., & Lu, H.-P. (2014). Assessment of institutions, scholars, and contributions on agile software development (2001–2012). *Journal of Systems and Software, 93*, 84–101. Retrieved from http://www.sciencedirect.com/science/article/pii/S01641212 14000697

Crowston, K., Rubleske, J., & Howison, J. (2006). Coordination theory: A ten-year retrospective. In P. Zhang & D. Galletta (Eds.), *Human-computer interaction in management information systems* (pp. 120–138). M. E. Sharpe, Inc.

Davis, S. M., & Lawrence, P. R. (1977). *Matrix.* Reading: Addison-Wesley.

Davison, R. B., Hollenbeck, J. R., Barnes, C. M., Sleesman, D. J., & Ilgen, D. R. (2012). Coordinated action in multiteam systems. *Journal of Applied Psychology, 97*(4), 808–824. Retrieved from http://www.ncbi.nlm.nih.gov/pubmed/22201246

DeChurch, L. A., & Marks, M. A. (2006). Leadership in multiteam systems. *Journal of Applied Psychology, 91*(2), 311–329. Retrieved from http://www.ncbi.nlm.nih.gov/pubmed/16551186

Deemer, P., Benefield, G., Larman, C., & Vodde, B. (2012). The Scrum primer version 2.0. Retrieved from http://www.scrumprimer.org/scrumprimer20_small.pdf

Devine, D. J. (2002). A review and integration of classification systems relevant to teams in organizations. *Group Dynamics: Theory, Research, and Practice, 6*(4), 291–310.

Dingsøyr, T., Fægri, T. E., & Itkonen, J. (2014). What is large in large-scale? A taxonomy of scale for agile software development. In A. Jedlitschka, P. Kuvaja, M. Kuhrmann, T. Männistö, J. Münch, & M. Raatikainen (Eds.), *Product-focused software process improvement* (Vol. 8892, pp. 273–276). Springer International Publishing. Retrieved from http://link.springer.com/10.1007/978-3-319-13835-0

Dingsøyr, T., & Moe, N. B. (2014). Towards principles of large-scale agile development. In T. Dingsøyr, N. Moe, R. Tonelli, S. Counsell, C. Gencel, & K. Petersen (Eds.), *Agile methods.*

Large-scale development, refactoring, testing, and estimation (Vol. 199, pp. 1–8). Springer International Publishing. Retrieved from http://www.springer.com/computer/swe/book/978-3-319-14357-6

Dybå, T., & Dingsøyr, T. (2008). Empirical studies of agile software development: A systematic review. *Information and Software Technology, 50*(9–10), 833–859. Retrieved from http://linkinghub.elsevier.com/retrieve/pii/S0950584908000256

Eckstein, J. (2014). Architecture in large scale agile development. In T. Dingsøyr, N. Moe, R. Tonelli, S. Counsell, C. Gencel, & K. Petersen (Eds.), *Agile methods. Large-scale development, refactoring, testing, and estimation* (Vol. 199, pp. 21–29). Springer International Publishing. Retrieved from http://dx.doi.org/10.1007/978-3-319-14358-3_3

Erdogmus, H., Morisio, M., & Torchiano, M. (2005). On the effectiveness of the test-first approach to programming. *IEEE Transactions on Software Engineering, 31*(3), 226–237.

Erickson, J., Lyytinen, K., & Siau, K. (2005). Agile modeling, agile software development, and extreme programming: The state of research. *Journal of Database Management, 16*(4), 88–100. Retrieved from http://www.igi-pub.com/articles/details.asp?ID=5327

Espinosa, J. A., Armour, F., & Boh, W. F. (2010). Coordination in enterprise architecting: An interview study. In *System Sciences (HICSS), 2010 43rd Hawaii International Conference on* (pp. 1–10).

Espinosa, J. A., Cummings, J. N., & Pickering, C. (2012). Time separation, coordination, and performance in technical teams. *IEEE Transactions on Engineering Management, 59*(1), 91–103.

Espinosa, J. A., Lerch, J. F., Kraut, R. E., Salas, E., & Fiore, S. M. (2004). Explicit vs. implicit coordination mechanisms and task dependencies: One size does not fit all. In *Team cognition: Understanding the factors that drive process and performance* (pp. 107–129). Washington, DC: American Psychological Association.

Faraj, S., & Xiao, Y. (2006). Coordination in fast-response organizations. *Management Science, 52*(8), 1155–1169. Retrieved from http://dx.doi.org/10.1287/mnsc.1060.0526

Fowler, M., & Highsmith, J. (2001). The agile manifesto. Retrieved from http://www.pmp-projects.org/Agile-Manifesto.pdf

Fry, C., & Greene, S. (2007). Large scale agile transformation in an on-demand world. In *Proceedings of the AGILE Conference 2007* (pp. 136–142). Washington, DC.

Goodhue, D. L., & Thompson, R. L. (1995). Task-technology fit and individual performance. *MIS Quarterly, 19*(2), pp. 213–236. Retrieved from http://www.jstor.org/stable/249689

Grzymala-Busse, A. (2010). Time will tell? Temporality and the analysis of causal mechanisms and processes. *Comparative Political Studies, 44*(9), 1267–1297. Retrieved from http://cps.sagepub.com/content/44/9/1267

Gulick, L., & Urwick, L. (1937). *Papers on the science of admininstration*. New York: Institute of Public Administration, Columbia University.

Guzzo, R. A., & Dickson, M. W. (1996). Teams in organizations: Recent research on performance and effectiveness. *Annual Review of Psychology, 47*(1), 307–338. Retrieved from http://dx.doi.org/10.1146/annurev.psych.47.1.307

Hempel, C. (1965). *Aspects of scientific explanation and other essays in the philosophy of science.* New York: The Free Press.

Hoda, R., Kruchten, P., Noble, J., & Marshall, S. (2010). Agility in context. In *Proceedings of the ACM International Conference on Object Oriented Programming Systems Languages and Applications* (pp. 74–88). New York, NY, USA: ACM. Retrieved from http://doi.acm.org/10.1145/1869459.1869467

Hole, S., & Moe, N. B. (2008). A case study of coordination in distributed agile software development. In R. O'Connor, N. Baddoo, K. Smolander, & R. Messnarz (Eds.), *Software process improvement* (Vol. 16, pp. 189–200). Springer Berlin Heidelberg. Retrieved from http://dx.doi.org/10.1007/978-3-540-85936-9_17

Hossain, E., Babar, M. A., & Paik, H. P. H. (2009). Using scrum in global software development: A systematic literature review. In *Global Software Engineering, 2009. ICGSE 2009. Fourth IEEE International Conference on* (pp. 175–184).

Ilgen, D. R., Hollenbeck, J. R., Johnson, M., & Jundt, D. (2004). Teams in organizations: From input-process-output models to IMOI models. *Annual Review of Psychology, 56*(1), 517–543. Retrieved from http://dx.doi.org/10.1146/annurev.psych.56.091103.070250

Jalali, S., & Wohlin, C. (2012). Global software engineering and agile practices: A systematic review. *Journal of Software: Evolution and Process, 24*(6), 643–659. Retrieved from http://dx.doi.org/10.1002/smr.561

Katz, D., & Kahn, R. L. (1978). *The social psychology of organizations*. Wiley.

Kettunen, P., & Laanti, M. (2008). Combining agile software projects and large-scale organizational agility. *Software Process: Improvement and Practice, 13*(2), 183–193. Retrieved from http://dx.doi.org/10.1002/spip.354

Kieser, A. (Ed.). (1993). *Organisationstheorien*. Kohlhammer.

Kotlarsky, J., van Fenema, P. C., & Willcocks, L. P. (2008). Developing a knowledge-based perspective on coordination: The case of global software projects. *Information & Management, 45*(2), 96–108.

Kozlowski, S. W. J., & Bell, B. S. (2003). Work groups and teams in organizations work groups and teams in organizations. In W. C. Borman, D. R. Ilgen, & R. J. Klimoski (Eds.), *Handbook of psychology: Industrial and organizational psychology* (Vol. 12, pp. 333–375). New York: Wiley.

Kraut, R. E., & Streeter, L. A. (1995). Coordination in software development. *Communications of the ACM, 38*(3), 69–81.

Kruchten, P. (1998). *The rational unified process: An introduction*. Amsterdam: Addison-Wesley Longman.

Laanti, M. (2014). Characteristics and principles of scaled agile. In T. Dingsøyr, N. Moe, R. Tonelli, S. Counsell, C. Gencel, & K. Petersen (Eds.), *Agile methods. Large-scale development, refactoring, testing, and estimation* (Vol. 199, pp. 9–20). Springer International Publishing. Retrieved from http://dx.doi.org/10.1007/978-3-319-14358-3_2

Lagerberg, L., Skude, T., Emanuelsson, P., Sandahl, K., & Stahl, D. (2013). The impact of agile principles and practices on large-scale software development projects: A multiple-case study of two projects at Ericsson. In *International Symposium on Empirical Software Engineering and Measurement* (pp. 348–356).

Lanaj, K., Hollenbeck, J. R., Ilgen, D. R., Barnes, C. M., & Harmon, S. J. (2012). The double-edged sword of decentralized planning in multiteam systems. *Academy of Management Journal, 56*(3), 1–61. Retrieved from http://amj.aom.org/content/early/2012/07/20/amj.2011.0350.short

Larman, C., & Basili, V. R. (2003). Iterative and incremental development: A brief history. *Computer, 36*(6), 47–56.

Larman, C., & Vodde, B. (2008). *Scaling lean & agile development: Thinking and organizational tools for large-scale Scrum*. Upper Saddle River, N.J: Addison-Wesley Professional.

Larman, C., & Vodde, B. (n.d.). LeSS Framework. Retrieved August 18, 2015, from http://less.works/

Lawrence, P. R., & Lorsch, J. W. (1967). Differentiation and integration in complex organizations. *Administrative Science Quarterly, 12*(1), 1–47. Retrieved from http://www.jstor.org/stable/2391211

Lee, E. C. (2008). Forming to performing: Transitioning large-scale project into agile. In *Agile 2008 Conference* (pp. 106–111). Toronto, ON.

Lee, G., Espinosa, J. A., & DeLone, W. (2013). Task environment complexity, global team dispersion, process capabilities, and coordination in software development. *IEEE Transactions on Software Engineering, 39*(12), 1753–1771.

Leffingwell, D. (n.d.). Scaled agile framework. Retrieved from http://www.scaledagileframework.com/

Li, Y., & Maedche, A. (2012). Formulating effective coordination strategies in agile global software development teams. In *Proceedings of the International Conference on Information Systems (ICIS 2012)* (pp. 1–6).

Malone, T. W., & Crowston, K. (1990). What is coordination theory and how can it help design cooperative work systems? In *Proceedings of the Conference on Computer Supported Cooperative Work*. Los Angeles.

Malone, T. W., & Crowston, K. (1991). Toward an interdisciplinary theory of coordination. *ACM Computing Surveys*, *120*(120), 1–45. Retrieved from http://dspace.mit.edu/handle/1721.1/2356

Malone, T. W., & Crowston, K. (1994). The interdisciplinary study of coordination. *ACM Computing Surveys*, *26*(1), 87–119. Retrieved from http://portal.acm.org/citation.cfm?doid= 174666.174668

Malone, T. W., Crowston, K., & Herman, G. A. (Eds.). (2003). *Organizing business knowledge: The MIT process handbook*. Cambridge, MA: MIT press.

Malone, T. W., Crowston, K., Lee, J., Pentland, B., Dellarocas, C., Wyner, G., … O'Donnell, E. (1999). Tools for inventing organizations: Toward a handbook of organizational processes. *Management Science*, *45*(3), 425–443. Retrieved from http://mansci.journal.informs.org/cgi/doi/10.1287/mnsc.45.3.425

Mangalaraj, G., Mahapatra, R., & Nerur, S. P. (2009). Acceptance of software process innovations —The case of extreme programming. *European Journal of Information Systems*, *18*(4), 344–354. Retrieved from http://www.palgrave-journals.com/ejis/journal/v18/n4/abs/ejis200923a.html

March, J. G., & Simon, H. A. (1958). *Organizations*. New York: Wiley.

Marks, M. A., DeChurch, L. A., Mathieu, J. E., Panzer, F. J., & Alonso, A. (2005). Teamwork in multiteam systems. *Journal of Applied Psychology*, *90*(5), 964–971. Retrieved from http://www.ncbi.nlm.nih.gov/pubmed/16162068

Marks, M. A., Mathieu, J. E., & Zaccaro, S. J. (2001). A temporally based framework and taxonomy of team processes. *The Academy of Management Review*, *26*(3), pp. 356–376. Retrieved from http://www.jstor.org/stable/259182

Mathieu, J. E., Marks, M. A., & Zaccaro, S. J. (2001). Multiteam systems. In N. Anderson, D. S. Ones, H. K. Sinangil, & C. Viswesvaran (Eds.), *Handbook of industrial, work and organizational psychology, Volume 2 Organizational psychology* (Vol. 2, pp. 289–313). London: Sage Publications Ltd.

Mathieu, J. E., & Maynard, M. T. (2008). Team effectiveness 1997–2007: A review of recent advancements and a glimpse into the future. *Journal of Management*, *34*(3), 410–476. Retrieved from http://jom.sagepub.com/cgi/doi/10.1177/0149206308316061

Mintzberg, H. (1980). Structure in 5's: A synthesis of the research on organization design. *Management Science*, *26*(3), 322–341. Retrieved from http://mansci.journal.informs.org/content/26/3/322.short

Mintzberg, H. (1983). *Structure in fives: Designing effective organizations*. Prentice-Hall, Inc.

Moe, N. B., Šmite, D., Šāblis, A., Börjesson, A.-L., & Andréasson, P. (2014). Networking in a large-scale distributed agile project. In *Proceedings of the 8th ACM/IEEE International Symposium on Empirical Software Engineering and Measurement* (pp. 12:1–12:8). New York, NY: ACM. Retrieved from http://doi.acm.org/10.1145/2652524.2652584

Moore, E., & Spens, J. (2008). Scaling agile: Finding your agile tribe. In *Agile 2008 Conference* (pp. 121–124). Toronto, ON.

Moreland, R., Argote, L., & Krishnan, R. (1996). Socially shared cognition at work: Transactive memory and group performance. In *What's social about social cognition? Research on socially shared cognition in small groups* (pp. 57–84). Sage Publications, Inc. Retrieved from http://psycnet.apa.org/psycinfo/1996-98278-003

Nerur, S. P., Mahapatra, R. K., & Mangalaraj, G. (2005). Challenges of migrating to agile methodologies. *Communications of the ACM, 48*(5), 72–78.

Nidumolu, S. (1995). The effect of coordination and uncertainty on software project performance: Residual performance risk as an intervening variable. *Information Systems Research, 6*(3), 191.

Nidumolu, S. (1996). A comparison of the structural contingency and risk-based perspectives on coordination in software-development projects. *Journal of Management Information System, 13*(2), 77–113. Retrieved from http://dl.acm.org/citation.cfm?id=1189558.1189564

Okhuysen, G. A., & Bechky, B. A. (2009). Coordination in organizations: An integrative perspective. *The Academy of Management Annals, 3*(1), 463–502.

Paasivaara, M., & Lassenius, C. (2011). Scaling scrum in a large distributed project. In *Empirical Software Engineering and Measurement (ESEM), 2011 International Symposium on* (pp. 363–367).

Paasivaara, M., Lassenius, C., & Heikkila, V. T. (2012). Inter-team coordination in large-scale globally distributed scrum: Do Scrum-of-Scrums really work? In *Empirical Software Engineering and Measurement (ESEM), 2012 ACM-IEEE International Symposium on* (pp. 235–238).

Paasivaara, M., Väättänen, O., Hallikainen, M., & Lassenius, C. (2014). Supporting a large-scale lean and agile transformation by defining common values. In T. Dingsøyr, N. Moe, R. Tonelli, S. Counsell, C. Gencel, & K. Petersen (Eds.), *Agile methods. Large-scale development, refactoring, testing, and estimation* (Vol. 199, pp. 73–82). Springer International Publishing. Retrieved from http://dx.doi.org/10.1007/978-3-319-14358-3_7

Pikkarainen, M., Haikara, J., Salo, O., Abrahamsson, P., & Still, J. (2008). The impact of agile practices on communication in software development. *Empirical Software Engineering, 13*(3), 303–337.

Poole, M. S., Van De Ven, A. H., Dooley, K., & Holmes, M. E. (2000). *Organizational change and innovation processes: Theory and methods for research.* Oxford University Press.

Power, K. (2014). A model for understanding when scaling agile is appropriate in large organizations. In T. Dingsøyr, N. Moe, R. Tonelli, S. Counsell, C. Gencel, & K. Petersen (Eds.), *Agile methods. Large-scale development, refactoring, testing, and estimation* (Vol. 199, pp. 83–92). Springer International Publishing. Retrieved from http://dx.doi.org/10.1007/978-3-319-14358-3_8

Rico, R., Sánchez-Manzanares, M., Gil, F., & Gibson, C. (2008). Team implicit coordination processes: A team knowledge-based approach. *Academy of Management Review, 33*(1), 163–184.

Royce, W. W. (1970). Managing the development of large software systems. In *Proceedings of IEEE WESCON* (Vol. 26, pp. 328–388).

Salas, E., Sims, D. E., & Burke, C. S. (2005). Is there a "big five" in teamwork? *Small Group Research, 36*(5), 555.

Scheerer, A., Bick, S., Hildenbrand, T., & Heinzl, A. (2015). The effects of team backlog dependencies on agile multiteam systems: A graph theoretical approach. In *System Sciences (HICSS), 2015 48th Hawaii International Conference on* (pp. 5124–5132). Koloa, HI. Retrieved from http://ieeexplore.ieee.org/document/7070428/

Scheerer, A., Hildenbrand, T., & Kude, T. (2014). Coordination in large-scale agile software development: A multiteam systems perspective. In *System Sciences (HICSS), 2014 47th Hawaii International Conference on* (pp. 4780–4788). Waikoloa, III. Retrieved from http://ieeexplore.ieee.org/document/6759189/

Schwaber, K., & Beedle, M. (2002). *Agile software development with Scrum.* Prentice Hall.

Schwaber, K., Dame, D., Hundhausen, R., Kong, P., Maher, R., Porter, S., ... Verheyen, G. (n.d.). Scaled Professional Scrum (Nexus) Framework. Retrieved August 21, 2015, from https://kenschwaber.files.wordpress.com/2015/06/nexusguide_v1-0.pdf

Schwaber, K., & Sutherland, J. (2013). The Scrum Guide. Retrieved from https://www.scrum.org/Portals/0/Documents/Scrum%20Guides/2013/Scrum-Guide.pdf

Simon, H. A. (1976). *Administrative behavior: A study of decision-making processes in administrative organization.* The Free Press.

Smits, H., & Pshigoda, G. (2007). Implementing scrum in a distributed software development organization. In *Agile Conference (AGILE), 2007* (pp. 371–375).

Strode, D. E., Hope, B., Huff, S. L., & Link, S. (2011). Coordination effectiveness in an agile software development context. In *PACIS 2011.*

Strode, D. E., Huff, S. L., Hope, B., & Link, S. (2012). Coordination in co-located agile software development projects. *Journal of Systems and Software, 85*(6), 1222–1238. Retrieved from http://dx.doi.org/10.1016/j.jss.2012.02.017

Sutherland, J., Schoonheim, G., & Rijk, M. (2009). Fully distributed scrum: Replicating local productivity and quality with offshore teams. In *System Sciences, 2009. HICSS'09. 42nd Hawaii International Conference on* (pp. 1–8).

Sutherland, J., & Schwaber, K. (1995). Business object design and implementation workshop. In *Addendum to the proceedings of the 10th annual conference on Object-oriented programming systems, languages, and applications (Addendum)* (pp. 170–175). New York, NY, USA: ACM. Retrieved from http://doi.acm.org/10.1145/260094.260274

Sutton, R. I., & Staw, B. M. (1995). What theory is not. *Administrative Science Quarterly, 40*(3), 371–384.

Takeuchi, H., & Nonaka, I. (1986). The new new product development game. *Harvard Business Review, 64*(1), 137–146. Retrieved from http://linkinghub.elsevier.com/retrieve/pii/0737678286900536

Tatikonda, M. V., & Rosenthal, S. R. (2000). Technology novelty, project complexity, and product development project execution success: A deeper look at task uncertainty in product innovation. *IEEE Transactions on Engineering Management, 47*(1), 74–87.

Taylor, F. W. (1911). *The principles of scientific management.* New York, London: Harper & Brothers.

Thompson, J. D. (1967). *Organizations in action: Social science bases of administrative theory* (Vol. 48). New York: McGraw-Hill.

Tosi, H. L. (2008). James March and Herbert Simon, Organizations. In *Theories of organization* (pp. 93–102). SAGE Publications, Inc.

Van De Ven, A. H., Delbecq, A. L., & Koenig, R. J. (1976). Determinants of coordination modes within organizations. *American Sociological Review, 41*(2), 322–338. Retrieved from http://www.jstor.org/stable/2094477

VersionOne Inc. (2013). 8th Annual State of Agile Development Survey. Retrieved from www.versionone.com/pdf/2013-state-of-agile-survey.pdf

Zaccaro, S. J., Marks, M. A., & DeChurch, L. A. (2012). Multiteam systems: An introduction. In S. J. Zaccaro, M. A. Marks, & L. A. DeChurch (Eds.), *Multiteam systems an organization form for dynamic and complex environments* (pp. 3–32). New York, NY, USA: Routledge.

Chapter 3
Research Design

The previous chapter depicted the foundations of this study, based on which the preliminary research framework was built. The following chapter presents the industrial research context of this study as well as the selection and specification of the research strategy. It finishes with the data collection and analysis procedures employed.

3.1 Research Context

The exploration of coordination configurations and their change over time was conducted at SAP SE (further referred to as 'SAP'), a multinational software development organization specializing on enterprise software. With more than 84,000 employees, customers in 190 countries and an annual revenue of more than 22 billion Euro, it is one of the largest enterprise software companies worldwide. Over 15,000 developers are currently working in the major development locations including Germany, United States, India, Bulgaria and China.

The history of agile software development at SAP started in 2004 with first experiments on Extreme Programming. A few teams decided to try agile practices but realized quickly that in a largely waterfall-based development organization this turned out to be increasingly difficult. Starting in 2006, a small team was formed to support development teams with the implementation of Scrum. Over the next two years, around 120 projects were completed with the Scrum method (Schnitter and Mackert 2010). The year 2012 marks the completion of the move to agile development methods in all of SAP's development areas (Scheerer et al. 2013).

© Springer International Publishing AG 2017
A. Scheerer, *Coordination in Large-Scale Agile Software Development*,
Progress in IS, DOI 10.1007/978-3-319-55327-6_3

3.1.1 Organizational Context

One major change was the introduction of Scrum as a process framework on the team level. Along with Scrum, there was no longer a 'project manager', but the roles of Scrum Master, responsible for the team process, and Product Owner, responsible for the product towards customers, were introduced.

Originating from small-scale settings (Schwaber and Beedle 2002), Scrum is not a perfect fit for large-scale development projects at first sight. Most of the development units at SAP, however, included several teams and comprised 150 developers and more. In the context of this industrial setting, the difference between 'project' and 'product' development became evident. Project development usually included a very limited amount of customers, often only one, and had a clear timeline when it would end. The teams staffed on such projects worked on them for a limited time and moved on to the next project once the previous was finished. Product development on the other hand, was based on the continuous implementation of a software product with mostly the same teams working on the software until it reached the end of its product life cycle. Some developers mentioned that they had essentially worked in the same team since they had started at SAP 15 years earlier. To cope with and benefit from this setting, an approach based on Larman and Vodde (2008, 2010) was implemented to scale Scrum for large software products.

Within this approach, the role of *Chief Product Owner* (CPO) was established. The CPO is responsible for an entire application or solution. Depending on the size of the product, there are usually one to two levels of *(Area) Product Owners* (APO), i.e. the overall product is divided into several 'product areas'. Within these teams, software developers, architects, user interface designers, documentation writers, etc. are working together to implement requirements.

The multiteam systems and the development teams contained therein are very heterogeneous with respect to technical characteristics (e.g. programming languages used, type of software developed), system setup (e.g. delivery or planning cycles) as well as organizational setup (e.g. component or feature orientation). These differing characteristics provide the diversity needed for the study at hand.

3.1.2 Embedded Research Setup

This research project had privileged access to the aforementioned company as the author worked as a research assistant at SAP between 2011 and 2015. During this time, he had the unique opportunity to gain deep insights into the issues under study in a real world professional software development setting. He further had the chance to join several trainings on development methodologies and contributed to SAP's agile efforts through various workshops with managers and developers alike. Over the course of the research project, additional exploratory studies focusing on different topics were conducted, which were outside the scope of the current study. Among them were interviews with 25 agile developers in five teams, network analyses of project management data from two multiteam systems, graph theoretical modelling of inter-team dependencies and countless informal talks with managers, technical experts and coaches. Some of these results have been published elsewhere (Scheerer et al. 2015, 2014, 2013).

In order to establish first insights into the problem space of inter-team work in large-scale agile development environments, an exploratory data analysis of the project management data of one product was carried out. A full release cycle was scrutinized in order to visualize and understand bottlenecks in the software development process. Overall, six months worth of data from more than 125 teams were examined. Through cumulative flow diagrams (Petersen and Wohlin 2011) and several interviews with employees responsible for continuous improvement, the underlying processes became apparent. A key finding was that strong mechanistic coordination alone could not mitigate interdependencies between teams. Four informal interviews with employees working together on another product (product management and developers) generated congruent insights. The management of dependencies, especially between teams, was the leading cause of problem escalations. The detailed results of this study have not been published, as organizational constraints did not allow for all research carried out to be made publicly available. However, the insights gained from this work formed the basis for the study at hand and strongly influenced the research strategy described in the following sections.

3.2   Selection of a Research Strategy

To answer the posed research questions, an appropriate research strategy must be chosen. Within the social sciences, researchers can choose from a plethora of differing research strategies including experimental, survey or case-based studies (Bhattacherjee 2012; Saunders et al. 2009).

A commonly used frame for the selection of a research strategy is based on three dimensions, the type of research question to be answered, if the study requires control of behavioral events and if a focus on contemporary events is necessary (Yin 2009). To these, Benbasat et al. (1987) add the established theoretical base of the researched phenomenon as another dimension.

The study's setting is in a large productive development organization with ongoing product development. This field environment does not lend itself to behavioral control in the form of experiments. Moreover, it is also not desirable to control the events under study, as this research wants to investigate and explore coordination in large-scale agile development systems in its natural setting, unaffected from outside influences. Furthermore, as agile development is a recent phenomenon the focus of this study is of a contemporary nature. Finally, the posed research question of this study is 'How do changes in the coordination configuration affect integrating conditions in multiteam software development systems?' with two sub questions (1) 'Why does the coordination configuration change?' and (2) 'How are the integrating conditions for coordination attained?'.

The how and why research questions together with the focus on contemporary events and the necessity to study these in their natural setting, strongly indicate the usage of the case study as a research strategy. Research in the field of agile software development is considered to be at a nascent to intermediate state (Dybå and Dingsøyr 2008; Hummel 2014). Based on this assessment, a qualitative case study approach (Yin 2009) seems particularly fitting as the research phenomenon is not supported by a strong theoretical base (Benbasat et al. 1987).

3.3   Specification of the Case Study Strategy

The inherent time-dependent nature of the research question in that it asks how changes affect software development systems, is the point of departure for pursuing a process theoretical approach (Mohr 1982).

In the realm of process theories concerned with organizational change and development, Poole et al. (2000) describe four types of theory inherent structures: evolution, dialectic, life cycle and teleology. These differ according to their unit and mode of change. Evolution, due to its premise of regarding change in populations, deals with multiple entities by definition. This change is of the prescribed variety, as forms are incrementally adapted in a pre-specified direction. Dialectic theories, also belonging to the multiple entities class, because of their need for at least two entities in the form of thesis and antithesis, are concerned with constructive change. This type of change produces new forms, which are often unpredictable based on previous forms. Life cycle and teleology theories deal with single entities and differ in their mode of change as life cycle views the entity as it progresses through different predefined cycle steps, while teleology, by its very nature, constructs change through the setting of new goals (Poole et al. 2000).

The research phenomenon investigated exhibits signs of constructive change, as coordination activities are conducted to achieve certain goals (e.g. new feature implementation or timely delivery) and a change to this type of process is a willful act in order to remedy some form of discontent. If a dissatisfaction with the current way of coordinating is present, new or alternative ways are searched for to reach the envisioned goals. The MTS as the unit of analysis is viewed as a single entity. According to Van de Ven and Poole (1995), this structure "can operate for an individual or for a group of individuals or organizations who are sufficiently like-minded to act as a single collective entity". This is the presumption concerning software product development teams, which have to work together in order to deliver one piece of software to customers. The single entity as the unit of change together with the constructive motor of change leads to this studies usage of the teleological type of process theory.

Underlying any scientific endeavor is an epistemological stance, a theory of knowledge that influences the chosen methodology and how a researcher views the data. Positivism, interpretivism and realism are a few examples of such positions (Chalmers 1999; Crotty 1998).

A positivist stance implies that an objective reality exists independent of the human mind (Orlikowski and Baroudi 1991). From this perspective, knowledge is created by experiences and observations of the world and depicts an objective and independent reality (Chalmers 1999). Interpretivism puts forth a view that reality is a product of social construction (Orlikowski and Baroudi 1991). Here, the reality and the researcher are of an inseparable nature where knowledge is intentionally constituted through the researcher's experience (Weber 2004).

This study follows a qualitative case study approach (Eisenhardt 1989) sometimes referred to as soft positivism (Kirsch 2004; Madill et al. 2000). As the nascent state of research in the field of agile software development (Dybå and Dingsøyr 2008; Hummel 2014) did not provide a strong theoretical base, this approach was employed in order to perform the data analysis with certain expectations based on available prior theory, but at the same time permitting some unexpected results and explanations to be derived from the data, closer to the interpretivist paradigm.

To increase the generalizability of the results, a multiple case study design was chosen, with the individual coordination configuration change process being the unit of analysis. In order to grasp the full spectrum of events that are likely to affect the evolution of changes in coordination configurations, a diverse sampling (Gerring 2007) approach was conducted. This matches the nature of the research, as mainly the generation of event sequences is of interest and not the testing of hypotheses. Within the software development company under study, the cases were selected based on varying the characteristics of the multiteam system (Zaccaro et al. 2012) to generate a heterogeneous sample (Poole et al. 2000). As such, five multiteam systems with differing sizes, delivery and planning cycles, as well as locations were identified for this study (see Table 3.1).

Table 3.1 Overall multiteam system demographics

	Alpha	Beta	Gamma	Delta	Epsilon	Total
Interviewees	23	22	9	7	5	66
CPO	1	2	–	1	1	5
APO	–	1	2	–	–	3
PO	11	8	–	5	4	28
SM	10	9	5	–	–	24
Other	1	2	2	1	–	6
Teams	13	9	7	6	4	39
Locations	4	2	6	1	3	–
Employees	~140	~95	~50	~85	~40	~410
Product type	On-premise	Cloud	On-premise and cloud	On-premise	On-premise and cloud	

3.4   Data Collection and Analysis Procedure

After having described the research and case study strategy in the previous sections, the following paragraphs will depict the data collection and analysis procedure in this research.

3.4.1   Data Collection

Data collection was divided into two phases. The first case data was gathered in October 2013, while the data from other cases was gathered between June 2014 and December 2014. Wherever possible, the interviews were held face-to-face. Interviews with remote partners were conducted via telephone, supported by collaborative tools (e.g. screen sharing).

Since change processes of coordination within multiteam systems are at the core of this study, interview partners in charge or with great knowledge of coordination within MTSs were chosen. In large-scale agile development, task coordination between teams lies mainly with the Product Owners and to a smaller extent with the Scrum Masters. The data was gathered by retrospective semi-structured interviews with Chief Product Owners in charge of the multiteam systems and the individual team Product Owners as well as Scrum Masters, Area Product Owners, architects (Arch) and other select roles (see Table 3.1). This retrospective approach made it possible to gather relevant coordination processes and changes to the multiteam system covering several months and at the same time minimizing data overload compared to a continuous longitudinal approach (Huber et al. 2013). Table 3.1 provides an overview of the multiteam systems investigated and their general demographics.

The interviews held were of a semi-structured nature (Kvale and Brinkmann 2009; Yin 2009). This type of interview is based on a skeleton in the form of an interview guideline to steer the conversation into the relevant direction. Nevertheless, the interviewee has the chance to speak openly and the researcher can veer from the guideline if interesting topics arise (Kvale and Brinkmann 2009). Based on the framework presented in Sect. 2.4.2, an interview guideline was developed to gain information concerning the context as well as aspects relevant to the coordination (see Appendix A Interview Guideline). To tease out coordination processes between teams, the Critical Incident Technique was utilized (Butterfield 2005; Flanagan 1954). The interviewees were asked to report on critical events where coordination between teams unfolded in a particularly successful or unsuccessful way. In doing so, the possibility of a cognitive bias was taken into account by asking about specific events instead of more general views. Using this question format, the participants were deliberately asked to think of specific events they experienced personally in the past, rather than describing their general perception of circumstances. Instead of asking could you describe situations where things often go wrong, they were asked to describe one particular situation in the past that they personally experienced. Questions 47 and 48 of the interview guideline (see Appendix A Interview Guideline) are exemplary to the posed questions within this technique.

Around 58 h of interviews were recorded with conversations lasting on average 40 minutes. This data was complemented by internal documentation and project management data available in the IT systems used for coordinating work in order to triangulate the data and increase internal validity (Yin 2009). All interviews were recorded and transcribed before the subsequent analysis. The transcriptions comprise more than 380,000 words (more than 1100 pages) of qualitative data. The data was then entered in computer assisted qualitative data analysis software (QSR NVivo 10) to help with the management and analysis of the empirical data collected.

In order to enhance the quality of the analysis, all responses and processes were additionally coded by a second researcher. The inter-rater agreement ratio (Dubé and Paré 2003) achieved between the two researchers was 74%. The remaining disagreements were discussed extensively to overcome discrepancies in the coding of the data and until an overall agreement could be reached.

3.4.2   Analysis of Process Changes

The single-case analysis of this study was guided by the research framework (see Sect. 2.5) with the individual change process of the coordination configuration as the unit of analysis. It followed an iterative three-stage process of data analysis outlined below (based on Huber et al. 2013).

Stage 1: Case story, Context and Network Analysis

This first stage included writing case stories for each analyzed multiteam system in order to gain an in-depth understanding of each case and its context as proposed by Miles and Huberman (1994). Supplementary sources in the form of wikis or other electronic documents were identified and investigated where available.

Based on the interview data and a coding scheme (see Appendix B Coding Schemes), sequential and reciprocal task dependencies (cf. Thompson 1967) between teams were identified and inserted into a dependency matrix for each case. Each of these matrices was then transferred into a directed graph, with reciprocal dependencies weighted double. From this directed graph, the in/out degree, betweenness centrality and strongly connected components were calculated and visualized (for definitions see Table 3.2). The result was a graphical representation of the team dependency structure of each MTS with the strongly connected components marked with colored slices. This helped in gaining an in-depth understanding of the contingency factor task dependencies that were present between teams in each MTS and formed the base for analyzing the trigger—change process— outcome episodes.

Table 3.2 Definitions of graph parameters

Parameter	Definition
In/out degree	The in-degree is the number of ingoing edges connected to a vertex and the out-degree is the number of outgoing edges (Newman 2010, p. 135)
Betweenness centrality	Measures the extent to which a vertex lies on paths between other vertices (Newman 2010, p. 185)
Strongly connected components	A strongly connected component is a maximal subset of vertices such that there is a directed path in both directions between every pair in the subset (Newman 2010, p. 144)
Density	The ratio of edges present in a graph to the maximum possible number of edges between vertices (Newman 2010, p. 134)
Diameter	The diameter of a graph is the length of the longest geodesic path between any pair of vertices in the network for which a path actually exists (Newman 2010, p. 140)

Stage 2: Analyzing Trigger—Change Process—Outcome Episodes

In the second stage the data was coded in NVivo based on a coding scheme (see Appendix B Coding Schemes). Every piece of process data was mapped to parts of the research framework. Starting with the triggering event and the initial integrating conditions, the changes in the coordination configuration and the final integrating conditions were identified in the interview data. Next, a representation in the form of a visual map was constructed for each process (Langley 1999). With the help of a second researcher the coding of process as well as all visual maps were discussed and compared until no discrepancies were present anymore.

Stage 3: Examining the Attainment of Integrating Conditions

In the final stage, a cross-case analysis was conducted to identify how the integrating conditions were attained. Coordination configurations were determined that acted as the source of the generated integrating conditions. In order to do so, all processes were reviewed and the originating coordination configuration was carved out for each final integrating condition of each process (see Appendix E Process Overview).

The types of coordination configurations and their relationship to the integrating conditions was analyzed based on contingency tables for which a chi-squared test of independence was performed. The null hypothesis $H_0 = coordination\ configurations\ are\ independent\ of\ the\ integrating\ conditions$ was established with the alternative hypothesis being that the coordination configurations and the integrating conditions have an association. However, sparsely populated contingency tables are a problem for Pearson's Chi-squared test of independence, in particular cells with an expected value of less than five lead to an incorrect approximation of the Chi-squared value (Hogg and Tanis 1996). To overcome this issue, another test was employed. An approach for small contingency tables is Fisher's exact test, which, as the name implies, calculates exact p-values.

The aspect of time was integrated next, through the examination of which integrating condition was generated in which process step (see Figs. 4.34, 4.35 and 4.36). It was towards the end of this stage that the findings were compared to the existing view on coordination.

Having presented the qualitative process theoretic research design of this study, the following chapter will describe the results of the multiple case study on coordination in multiteam systems.

References

Benbasat, I., Goldstein, D. K., & Mead, M. (1987). The case research strategy in studies of information systems. *MIS Quarterly, 11*(3), 369–386.

Bhattacherjee, A. (2012). Social science research: Principles, methods, and practices. *USF Open Access Textbooks Collection*, Book 3.

Butterfield, L. D. (2005). Fifty years of the critical incident technique: 1954–2004 and beyond. *Qualitative Research, 5*(4), 475–497.

Chalmers, A. F. (1999). *What is this thing called science?* (3rd revise). Hackett Publishing Company.

Crotty, M. J. (1998). *The foundations of social research: Meaning and perspective in the research process.* SAGE Publications Ltd.

Dubé, L., & Paré, G. (2003). Rigor in information systems positivist case research: Current practices, trends, and recommendations. *MIS Quarterly, 27*(4), 597–636. Retrieved from http://www.jstor.org/stable/30036550

Dybå, T., & Dingsøyr, T. (2008). Empirical studies of agile software development: A systematic review. *Information and Software Technology, 50*(9–10), 833–859. Retrieved from http://linkinghub.elsevier.com/retrieve/pii/S0950584908000256

Eisenhardt, K. M. (1989). Building theories from case study research. *The Academy of Management Review, 14*(4), 532–550. Retrieved from http://www.jstor.org/stable/258557

Flanagan, J. C. (1954). The critical incident technique. *Psychological Bulletin, 51*(4), 327–358.

Gerring, J. (2007). *Case study research: Principles and practices. Social Science* (Vol. 1). Cambridge University Press.

Hogg, R. V., & Tanis, E. A. (1996). *Probability and statistical inference* (5th ed.). Prentice Hall.

Huber, T. L., Fischer, T. a., Dibbern, J., & Hirschheim, R. (2013). A process model of complementarity and substitution of contractual and relational governance in IS outsourcing. *Journal of Management Information Systems, 30*(3), 81–114.

Hummel, M. (2014). State-of-the-art: A systematic literature review on agile information systems development. In *System Sciences (HICSS), 2014 47th Hawaii International Conference on* (pp. 4712–4721).

Kirsch, L. J. (2004). Deploying common systems globally: The dynamics of control. *Information Systems Research, 15*(4), 374–395.

Kvale, S., & Brinkmann, S. (2009). *Interviews: Learning the craft of qualitative research interviewing.* Los Angeles, CA: Sage.

Langley, A. (1999). Strategies for theorizing from process data. *The Academy of Management Review, 24*(4), 691–710.

Larman, C., & Vodde, B. (2008). *Scaling lean & agile development: Thinking and organizational tools for large-scale Scrum.* Upper Saddle River, NJ: Addison-Wesley Professional.

Larman, C., & Vodde, B. (2010). *Practices for scaling lean and agile development: Large, multisite, and offshore product development with large-scale scrum* (1st ed.). Upper Saddle River, NJ: Addison-Wesley Professional.

Madill, A., Jordan, A., & Shirley, C. (2000). Objectivity and reliability in qualitative analysis: Realist, contextualist and radical constructionist epistemologies. *British Journal of Psychology*, *91*(1), 1–20. Retrieved from http://dx.doi.org/10.1348/000712600161646

Miles, M. B., & Huberman, A. M. (1994). *Qualitative data analysis: An expanded sourcebook* (2nd ed.). Sage Publications, Inc.

Mohr, L. B. (1982). *Explaining organizational behavior*. San Francisco: Jossey-Bass.

Newman, M. (2010). *Networks: An introduction*. Oxford University Press.

Orlikowski, W. J., & Baroudi, J. J. (1991). Studying information technology in organizations: Research approaches and assumptions. *Information Systems Research, 2*(1), 1–28.

Petersen, K., & Wohlin, C. (2011). Measuring the flow in lean software development. *Software Practice and Experience, 41*(9), 975–996. Retrieved from http://dx.doi.org/10.1002/spe.975

Poole, M. S., Van De Ven, A. H., Dooley, K., & Holmes, M. E. (2000). *Organizational change and innovation processes: Theory and methods for research*. Oxford University Press.

Saunders, M., Lewis, P., & Thornhill, A. (2009). *Research methods for business students*. Prentice-Hall.

Scheerer, A., Bick, S., Hildenbrand, T., & Heinzl, A. (2015). The effects of team backlog dependencies on agile multiteam systems: A graph theoretical approach. In *System Sciences (HICSS), 2015 48th Hawaii International Conference on* (pp. 5124–5132). Koloa, HI. Retrieved from http://ieeexplore.ieee.org/document/7070428/

Scheerer, A., Hildenbrand, T., & Kude, T. (2014). Coordination in large-scale agile software development: A multiteam systems perspective. In *System Sciences (HICSS), 2014 47th Hawaii International Conference on* (pp. 4780–4788). Waikoloa, HI. Retrieved from http://ieeexplore.ieee.org/document/6759189/

Scheerer, A., Schmidt, C. T., Heinzl, A., Hildenbrand, T., & Voelz, D. (2013). Agile software engineering techniques: The missing link in large scale lean product development. In S. Kowalewski & B. Rumpe (Eds.), *Lecture Notes in Informatics (LNI)—Proceedings of the SE2013* (Vol. P-213, pp. 319–330).

Schnitter, J., & Mackert, O. (2010). Introducing agile software development at SAP AG— Change procedures and observations in a global software company. In *Proceedings of the 5th International Conference on Evaluation of Novel Approaches to Software Engineering (ENASE)*.

Schwaber, K., & Beedle, M. (2002). *Agile software development with Scrum*. Prentice Hall.

Thompson, J. D. (1967). *Organizations in action: Social science bases of administrative theory* (Vol. 48), New York: McGraw-Hill.

Van de Ven, A. H., & Poole, M. S. (1995). Explaining development and change. *The Academy of Management Review, 20*(3), 510–540.

Weber, R. (2004). Editor's comments: The rhetoric of positivism versus interpretivism: A personal view. *MIS Quarterly, 28*(1), iii–xii.

Yin, R. K. (2009). *Case study research: Design and methods* (4th ed.). Sage Publications, Inc.

Zaccaro, S. J., Marks, M. A., & DeChurch, L. A. (2012). Multiteam systems: An introduction. In S. J. Zaccaro, M. A. Marks, & L. A. DeChurch (Eds.), *Multiteam systems an organization form for dynamic and complex environments* (pp. 3–32). New York, NY: Routledge.

Chapter 4
Case Study Results on Coordination in Multiteam Systems

This chapter presents the results of the conducted case study on coordination in multiteam systems. The first part in Sect. 4.1 introduces a single-case analysis of each of the five cases in this study with their respective MTS structure, dependencies and coordination as well as the coordination configuration change processes. The second part in Sect. 4.2 presents a cross-case analysis wherein the cause for coordination configuration changes and an analysis of the attainment of the integrating conditions for coordinated action is presented.

4.1 Single-Case Analysis

What follows are the insights gained from the analysis of each individual case. As outlined in Sect. 3.4, the following presents the outcome of the single-case analysis. Each multiteam system is introduced before its individual contextual factors are shown. The MTS structure, team dependencies and coordination aspects are described. As it is inherently difficult to scale coordination from small to large-scale settings (Barlow et al. 2011), the agile method scaling approach or the way in which the MTSs adapted agile to their individual settings is presented. Finally, the change processes within each case are depicted in detail.

To illustrate these processes in a comparable manner, a unified representation was developed, which is explained in Fig. 4.1. The processes start out with a triggering event, illustrated in the oval form on the top. The initial integrating conditions that were present at the time of the trigger are depicted in the box below. In Fig. 4.1, the integrating condition common understanding was lacking, indicated by the hollow circle before it. The filled circle before accountability illustrates the presence of this condition. If no circle is present in the integrating conditions, these were not relevant for this process (e.g. predictability in this case). The change process is portrayed on the right, where several coordination configurations are plotted vertically. These give a picture of how the configurations evolved over time.

© Springer International Publishing AG 2017
A. Scheerer, *Coordination in Large-Scale Agile Software Development*,
Progress in IS, DOI 10.1007/978-3-319-55327-6_4

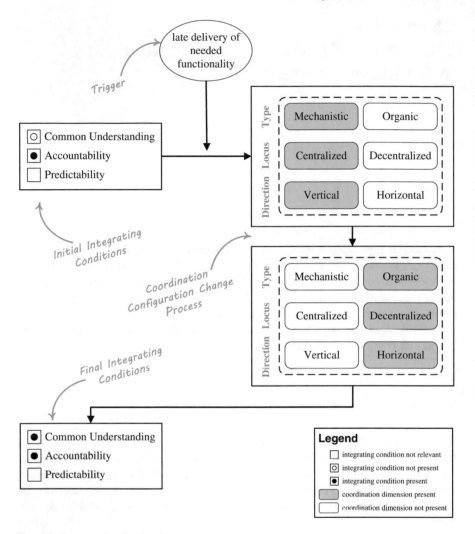

Fig. 4.1 Process visualization key

The boxes shaded in grey show which of the three dimensions, type, locus and direction, were present. Lastly, the box on the bottom left describes the final integrating conditions present after the change process was concluded.

4.1.1   Case Alpha

The first of the five cases investigated is MTS *Alpha*, which was developing a logistics solution with 13 teams in four locations (see Table 4.1). This solution had

Table 4.1 Case alpha characteristics

Teams	13
Locations	4
Employees	~140
Product type	On-premise
Avg. Company Tenure	12 years
Avg. MTS Tenure	5 years
Avg. Team Tenure	4 years
Avg. Role Tenure	3 years
Product maturity	>10 years
Customer delivery	~12 months
Team sprint length	4 weeks
Product complexity	High
Requirements uncertainty	Low-medium
Inter-team coordination responsibility	Central Team, PO

been in development for more than 10 years with around 140 employees involved in the multiteam system. The product had attracted many customers across a diversified field, which it supported. Due to the wide range of customers with their diverse requirements, the underlying business process was very complex. The result of this was a high product complexity, as rated by the interview participants. Due to the many aspects that were regulated in the logistics industry, the uncertainty of requirements was seen as low-medium. The needed functionality that the customers demanded seemed to be evident yet very comprehensive, although all details were seldom clear from the beginning. Additionally, the high-level requirements did not change often. The on-premise software product was characterized as being a tightly integrated system with almost no requirements that could be implemented within one single team.

4.1.1.1 MTS Structure, Dependencies and Coordination

The development teams within this multiteam system were divided according to the process steps supported by the product they were developing. Due to the complex and broad domain knowledge needed to develop this solution, the teams were each specialized on certain aspects of the underlying business process (e.g. invoicing). The composition of each team covered all aspects of the software stack including a user interface expert, quality testing engineers, and architecture specialists.

The solution stemmed from the traditional large enterprise on-premise world, where customers were hesitant to update their mission critical enterprise software hastily. As such, new releases of the product were delivered to the customer approximately every 12 months, which represents a formidable reduction of the release cycle that previously was considerably longer. Based on this long-term perspective, the high-level release planning looked several years ahead. On the inter-team level, the upcoming sprints of four weeks were planned in a cycle of three months.

In general, the teams had little autonomy concerning the development topics. A central team compiled the higher-level work items (epics) and pushed these to the individual teams. The central team was staffed with employees outside of the teams.

Interviewee 32: "Content wise, the work items are rather prescribed through the central team. [...] So we have relatively little freedom concerning that."
Interviewee 1: "Well, we have minimal empowerment. Essentially, the backlog items are tossed in from above. So, there is a central team which thinks about the next things which should be done and that is then defined."

Interestingly, one team mentioned their independence from this central team due to the new nature of their development topic and their direct and close interaction with the customer.

Interviewee 5: "[...] as I have meetings with customers three to ten times a week where I talk about the requirements with them, I decide what is done in the next sprint. I present that to the central team, so that they now what is going on. Until now they have always agreed to my suggestions."

To manage task allocation and establish a minimal form of status transparency, a common backlog management tool was promoted, but its usage varied heavily. Some teams used it very consistently while others decided to use it minimally and continue their team planning in other office tools. In addition, a comprehensive wiki was cultivated with current information on the general setup of the multiteam system and material on technical and administrative aspects.

The inter-team dependencies depicted in Fig. 4.2 show many one-way sequential dependencies, which depicts the existence of producer-consumer relationships between the teams. The large slice illustrates the tightly integrated core teams, with several reciprocal dependencies between four teams. In contrast to this cluster, the four individual teams can be viewed as service teams. These teams show little to no sequential dependencies toward other teams and could act more independently than the rest of the system in order to fulfill their requirements. These service teams implemented modules with self-contained features and relied only on data structures from the main teams.

Looking at the parameters of the task dependency graph, the density figure of case Alpha is the lowest in comparison to the other cases (see Table 4.2). This can be explained through the high overall number of teams within the MTS relative to the lower number of core development teams. Those four teams that were not part of the one large strongly connected component were acting as service teams to the core component teams. With these almost external service providing teams, few dependencies existed. Within the largest strongly connected component, however, the core teams were much more heavily connected, which would—if adjusted to the number of core teams—then lead to a higher value of overall density. The

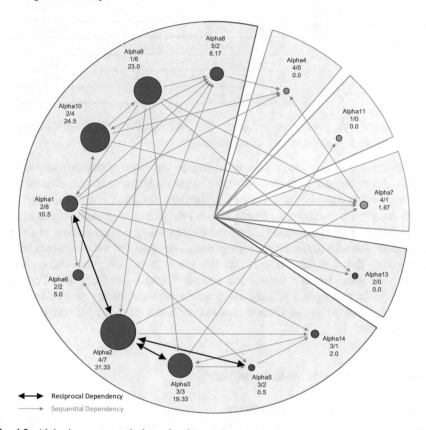

Fig. 4.2 Alpha inter-team task dependencies

parameter diameter is also the largest in case Alpha, which underscores the tightly integrated software built by Alpha and the fact that very few features could be implemented by only one team. Regarding the betweenness centrality, or the extent to which a vertex lies on paths between other vertices (see definitions in Table 3.2), case Alpha stands out once more, as many of the core teams' nodes have a very high betweenness centrality, depicted by the node size. An overview of all graph parameters across the five MTSs is provided in the Appendix C Network Analysis Results (for parameter definitions see Table 3.2).

The general coordination style within this multiteam system can be characterized as top-down. A central team came up with high-level epics and assigned a lead team to each, based on which team fits best to the topic. Initial dependencies were specified but many times not all were discovered. The assigned lead team then had to detail out the epic and coordinate with other teams in case input from them was needed. The discovery of further dependencies and delivery timeline discussions with other teams also fell into the hands of the lead team. Often, discussions between teams did not lead to any resolution, and were then escalated back up to the central team.

Table 4.2 Case alpha graph parameters

Graph Parameter	Value
# Strongly connected components	5
Average degree	2.692
Density	0.231
Diameter	5

Interviewee 7: "[…] we steer rather central and top-down. We aren't bottom-up, we are clearly top-down in our management."

From the examined data, a new condition in the form of transparency became evident. An open and proactive communication culture concerning current problems and background information or explanations for decisions taken were mentioned, essentially the aspects of problem and decision transparency came to light. Workload and progress transparency was mentioned as a critical item in order to assess the status of individual teams from a team-to-team and a team-to-central team perspective. The definition adopted in this research is "the perceived quality of intentionally shared information from a sender" (Schnackenberg and Tomlinson 2014, p. 5). In this light, the integrating condition transparency was added to the research framework and examined together with the three established conditions from literature.

4.1.1.2   Agile Method Scaling Approach

Scaling via Central Team Directives

One way to cope with the increased difficulty of coordinating a large number of teams and employees is to install an entity specifically for that purpose. In case Alpha, the central team is an example of such an approach. Seven people, including the CPO, architects and product experts, formed this team, which generated the high-level work items in the form of epics and allocated them to a lead development team. The central team met daily for one hour to discuss current and pressing topics as well as to plan the upcoming sprints. This team was a separate entity to the development teams in the multiteam system and did not include any team representatives.

Once per sprint, the central team hosted a status and handover meeting with each of the development teams individually. In this meeting, the central team wanted to see what was achieved by the development team in the last sprint and to communicate what the backlog items and their priorities for the next sprint were.

The scaling approach via a central team dealt with the matter of team interlocks due to priority conflicts.

Interviewee 7: "An issue which we could address through the introduction of the central team was the mutual blocking of teams. Because they are strongly interconnected, we previously often had the situation that priority 1 from one team was priority 3 of the next team and these two teams actually had to work together."

However, not all members of the multiteam system were positive about this setup.

Interviewee 7: "The POs normally don't like this solution, because we restrict the responsibility a PO has considerably [...]."

Another consequence of this approach seemed to be that the central team could not foresee all dependencies between teams, which led to recurring escalations to solve resulting issues.

Interviewee 7: "[...] usually we can't anticipate all the dependencies between teams in the central team."

Finally, responsibility for inter-team coordination was relocated to the central team.

Interviewee 11: "[...] we always inform to one group of people [the central team] and it is up to them to talk to the others."

This also led to a centralized problem solving strategy, where the central team was generally called upon to settle disputes.

Interviewee 43: "[...] so we wouldn't have planned for it [a backlog item from another team], somehow the other team would escalate and we would end up spending time on the topic which we have not planned, because a combination of the local management here and then the central team decided."

The perceived quality of coordination was heterogeneous. While some interviewees saw room for improvement or rated it as acceptable, others considered the coordination within their multiteam system as highly problematic.

4.1.1.3 Change Processes

Alpha-P1 Unclear Mutual Expectations
In the first coordination configuration change process *Alpha-P1* (see Fig. 4.3), unclear mutual expectations acted as a catalyst to reveal missing common understanding that led to a change of the configuration from very organic, decentral and horizontal to purely mechanistic and centralized.

Interviewee 5: "[...] it wasn't exactly clear what was wanted or what was needed [...] at some point it becomes apparent that something isn't right. [...] We escalate [...] have meetings and reprioritize [...]."

An interviewee of MTS Alpha reported an incident where his team needed a delivery of functionality from another team. During development, interviewee 5's team became aware of the fact that the delivery did not fit to what was needed. This issues was then escalated to the central team, which actively got involved in the discussion between the two teams. The lack of knowledge about the needed

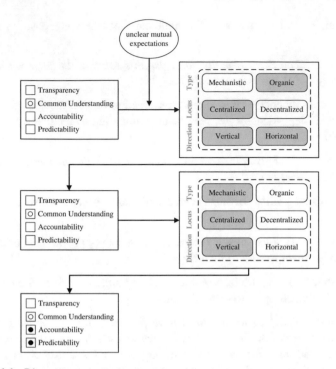

Fig. 4.3 Alpha-P1 process

functionality indicates a lack of common understanding, which resulted in the depicted dependency conflict. By stepping in and taking mechanistic measures in the form of plan adaptation and reprioritization, the central team centralized the coordination and resolved the situation.

The integrating conditions present after the process were accountability and predictability, because the central team reprioritized and adapted the plan. However, no common understanding was present, as the involved teams did not come to an agreement concerning the issue.

Alpha-P2 Lacking Knowledge of Another Team's Activities
The process *Alpha-P2* (see Fig. 4.4) was initially set off because some teams were not aware of another team's activities. This uncovered a lack of transparency and common understanding across several teams. These lacking conditions led to a situation where an organic and decentralized configuration switched completely to a mechanistic and centralized one. Interviewee 1 described a circumstance where his team had built new functionality and had assumed that the other teams that were affected by the implementation had already considered the changes in their tasks. This had not been the case and caused a direct escalation to the central team. They in turn obliged the involved teams to take care of this requirement and deliver what was still needed in order to finish the requirement.

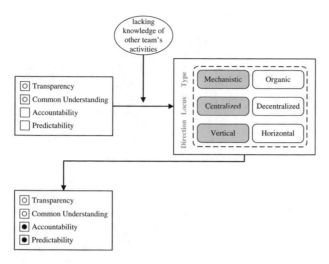

Fig. 4.4 Alpha-P2 process

Interviewee 1: "[...] team 1 builds something and somehow it is forgotten to talk with team 2 and 3 and in the end something doesn't work because somebody expected that the requirement, which was built by team 1, is also taken into consideration in the other teams."

Since no change in the teams' information sharing behavior was undertaken and both teams did not increase their understanding of the topic, neither condition was present after the change process. However, accountability and predictability existed as the central team assigned work items to the teams and communicated due dates.

Alpha-P3 Unknown Dependencies Between Teams
The absence of transparency and common understanding was also the case in process *Alpha-P3* (see Fig. 4.5). Here, unknown dependencies between teams exposed the lack of the two conditions that caused a change in the configuration. The central team assigned a plan to a lead team, which discovered that other teams would have to deliver new functionality in order to implement that requirement. The other teams did not have time to do this and would not commit to the plan. This deadlock situation was then communicated to the central team, which got involved in the discussion. The blocked topic was stopped while the discussions were ongoing in order to reprioritize or stop the blocking topics.

Interviewee 7: "Often we think that topics are independent and give them to the teams only to have the experts come back to us and tell us, if we should implement this then another team has to implement something first and the other team doesn't have time right know. We have that sort of problem a lot."

The final integrating condition present was common understanding, as the discussions among the teams and the central team led to a better perception of the

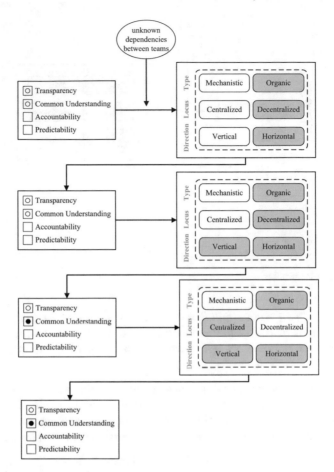

Fig. 4.5 Alpha-P3 process

backlog items among all participants. Transparency was not affected, because no sustainable changes were implemented to be aware of such dependencies in the future.

Alpha-P4 Increase in Geographic Dispersion

The process *Alpha-P4* (see Fig. 4.6) depicts a loss of integrating conditions for coordination due to an increase in geographic distance. The PO of one of the teams had to undertake work travel. Previously, the other team and this PO had a daily sync call early in the morning. During the PO's absence, the daily calls had stopped and after returning, the practice was not reestablished. Instead of a call, the other team sent a daily status e-mail to inform what had been done the previous day. The information shared with the Product Owner decreased and no opportunity for questions was possible.

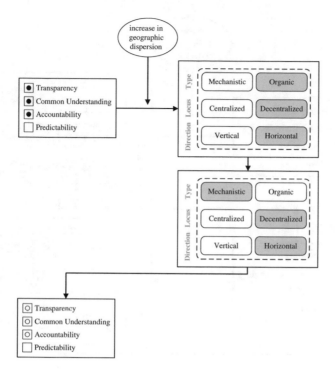

Fig. 4.6 Alpha-P4 process

All three integrating conditions present in the beginning became absent during the course of this change process.

Alpha-P5 Corruption of Shared Codebase
The lack of accountability in process *Alpha-P5* (see Fig. 4.7) became evident through the corruption of a shared codebase between two teams. The search for the cause of this corruption led to a finger-pointing situation between the two teams with no resolution of the issue possible. The involved POs and SMs discussed how to mitigate such situations in the future and created a regular Scrum Master sync, where this kind of issue could be reported.

Interviewee 58: "[...] we came to the conclusion that we should have a Scrum Master sync, so the team doesn't come to a pointing at each other situation, rather you would inform the Scrum Master and in the Scrum Master sync we bring this up and try to check out if this really is an issue or if this is a showstopper type of issue and we look into it."

In the course of this process, due to the creation of resolution mechanism which could be used in the future the integrating condition accountability was established in a sustainable manner.

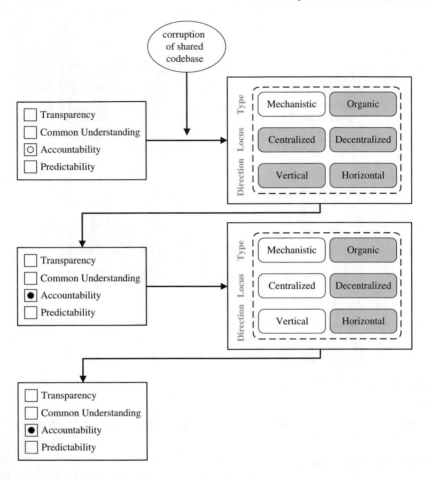

Fig. 4.7 Alpha-P5 process

Alpha-P6 Work Item Spanning Across Teams

The process *Alpha-P6* (see Fig. 4.8) shows the establishment of all integrating conditions. A new work item was pushed from the central team to a lead team. As this item included work for which several teams had to be involved, one team became the designated lead team and was responsible for the coordination of the work between the involved teams. The lead PO established a daily synchronization call for the duration of the implementation between the teams to discuss priorities and current issues.

Interviewee 61: "He [the PO] made sure that we had a daily sync call across three locations. Every day, we used to discuss 'these are the top priority issues that need to be solved". [...] It was good, because everybody was on the same page. Everybody knew what issues were of top priority and what everybody needed to work on. This daily sync call was really effective [...]."

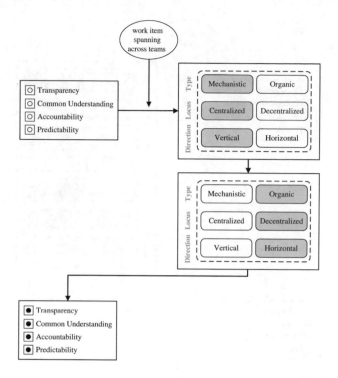

Fig. 4.8 Alpha-P6 process

Through this sync call, transparency was established as all involved teams reported their status and issues. Common understanding was created within the discussions of how to implement certain requirements and accountability and predictability was formed in direct communication among the teams.

Alpha-P7 Unclear Work Items
The lack of common understanding, accountability and predictability in process *Alpha-P7* (see Fig. 4.9) was uncovered after the assignment of unclear work items by the central team. The teams that were supposed to implement the functionality did not comprehend the requirements. This led to multiple meetings across the hierarchy including the central team. These meetings were needed in order to clarify and prioritize work items. Finally, common understanding and accountability was created through these discussions, but predictability could not be established, as the implementation took longer than expected.

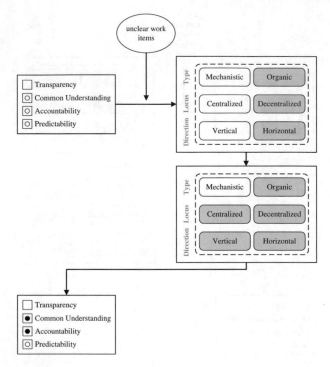

Fig. 4.9 Alpha-P7 process

4.1.2 Case Beta

The second case in this analysis is a multiteam system called *Beta*, which was developing an integration platform to connect on-premise systems with cloud solutions. This MTS consisted of nine teams with around 95 employees spread across two locations (see Table 4.3). The development of this product had been carrying on for more than five years. In contrast to case Alpha, the business process complexity underlying this solution was lower, however, the technical complexity was rated much higher. This lead to an overall assessment by the interviewees of a medium-high product complexity. Most of the requirements, as they were of a technical nature, were known and did not change during the development phases. This resulted in low-medium requirements uncertainty evaluation by the interview partners. In line with the more technical focus of this product, the software architecture was modularized along the technical components needed for the integration services provided by the solution.

Table 4.3 Case beta
characteristics

Teams	9
Locations	2
Employees	~95
Product type	Cloud
Avg. Company Tenure	11 years
Avg. MTS Tenure	4 years
Avg. Team Tenure	_[a]
Avg. Role Tenure	2 years
Product maturity	>5 years
Customer delivery	1 month
Team sprint length	2 weeks
Product complexity	Medium-high
Requirements uncertainty	Low-medium
Inter-team coordination responsibility	PO, SM

[a]Not enough data was available to calculate this figure

4.1.2.1 MTS Structure, Dependencies and Coordination

The team structure in case Beta was originally based on the technical components of the software. Starting in 2014 however, most of the teams had transitioned to a feature team approach (Larman and Vodde 2008) and could implement customer features along the entire software stack. Each team retained parts of their original component responsibility, as the technical expertise was the greatest among those teams.

The product was delivered to the customer every four weeks with high-level planning covering a period of three months. The detailed sprint planning by each of the teams was carried out for the next four weeks with individual sprints lasting two weeks.

The development teams had a large degree of autonomy as the team Product Owners gathered in a monthly CPO/PO round. This round was a regular meeting that included the two Chief Product Owners and the individual team Product Owners. Within this virtual team, the members gathered to discuss system-wide requirements, cross-team topics and priorities as well as potential dependencies. Decisions which affected the teams and the overall product were taken here and an implementation plan was derived.

Interviewee 36: "We can plan small scale improvements on our own, but larger ones need to be agreed upon in the PO round. Through me as a PO the team has influence on that as well. So, I always ask the team, 'what should we do? What do you view as useful?' I take those suggestions up and bring them into the PO round."

Throughout the entire MTS, a common backlog management tool was advocated and its usage was uniformly high across the multiteam system. On top of that, a

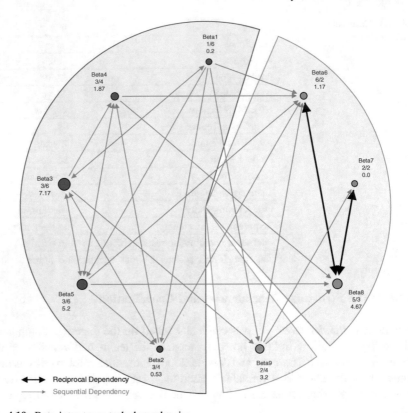

Fig. 4.10 Beta inter-team task dependencies

comprehensive wiki was cultivated with current information on the general setup of the multiteam system, their definition of done and material on technical and administrative aspects.

Figure 4.10 shows the inter-team task dependencies for the MTS Beta. This graph shows a balanced amount of dependencies compared to the number of teams. Some two-way sequential relationships can be seen (e.g. between Beta 3 and 5). What becomes very apparent is a division in foundation teams and user interface (UI) teams. Teams 6-9 built the UI layer for this solution. Beta 9 built a foundation layer for the other UI teams, which explains the individual assignment into one component with sequential dependencies to the other UI teams. In contrast to case Alpha, where only the core teams show a high density of dependencies, in case Beta almost all teams have several dependencies towards other teams (higher average degree) (see Table 4.4). The general coordination style was a mixed and collaborative approach with high-level planning originating from the Chief Product Owners and bottom-up proposals coming from the teams.

Interviewee 57: "I cannot differentiate completely whether it is top-down or bottom-up. It is a mixed approach, which we take."

Table 4.4 Case beta graph parameters

Graph parameter	Value
# Strongly connected components	3
Average degree	3.111
Density	0.389
Diameter	3

The planning process within Beta is best described by one of the interviewees:

Interviewee 36: "In the middle of the takt,[1] *the CPOs call for input from the team POs. As a team, we collect requirements and through the CPOs, requirements come in as well. Every team PO sends his topics for the next takt to the CPOs and to the other POs. We then discuss those topics in the CPO/PO round. Each team PO should call attention to dependencies, so to topics which need input from other teams. This is then discussed to the last detail in the PO round. At the end of the takt the topics are sorted according to their priority, so that the POs know what the CPOs priorities are for the next takt."*

When facing problems or other unplanned events, the development teams of Beta followed a clear process to resolve those issues. The involved team POs would discuss among themselves and come to a resolution, which was then communicated to the CPOs and the other team POs.

4.1.2.2   Agile Method Scaling Approach

Scaling via Iterative Proxy Collaboration
MTS Beta chose an approach which is close to the Scrum of Scrums method described in literature (Larman and Vodde 2010). Representatives of each team met up on the next higher level of the hierarchy and formed a virtual central team. As such, Beta had a CPO/PO round consisting of the two CPOs and all POs of the development teams. This virtual team met regularly to discuss the upcoming sprint and plan, which backlog items were to be developed. Disputes and coordination problems, which could not be solved directly between teams, were resolved in this group.

In the middle of the current sprint, the CPOs gathered new topics for the next sprint from the POs. These were discussed in the aforementioned CPO/PO round and discussed in detail, explicitly considering dependencies to other teams. As the team POs were already part of the planning process from the beginning no explicit handover meeting was necessary.

---

[1]In the MTS Beta, two sprints formed a so called 'takt'. The takt served as the MTS-wide synchronization and integration point.

If problems arose during the implementation phase, a defined process was followed. The team POs discussed the issue among themselves and came up with a solution. This solution was then communicated to the CPOs who had to accept the proposal.

Interviewee 36: "If something unexpected happens in the development sprint, we have to file a change request to the CPOs and mail it around to the other POs so that everybody knows that something has changed and it could affect other teams as well."

Among the interviewed, the overall satisfaction with the coordination was very high.

Interviewee 51: "Generally speaking it [the coordination] is working well."
Interviewee 57: "I think it's pretty well managed."

4.1.2.3   Change Processes

Beta-P1 Missing Communication of Decommitment
Interviewee 66 described a situation in process *Beta-P1* (see Fig. 4.11), where the absence of transparency and predictability was noticed through the missing communication of a decommitment of backlog items. His team had relied on a delivery of functionality from another team to finish their current backlog items within the sprint. The needed functionality was promised to be delivered in the current sprint. However, a more important issue arose in the second team, which prevented this team to fulfill the request. This decommitment was not communicated to interviewee 66's team and led to a delay in his team's delivery of backlog items, as they could not be finished within the sprint in which they were started. To prevent such situations from happening in the future, a discussion among the POs and CPOs was initiated subsequent to this circumstance. It was decided to establish a regular synchronization meeting between POs to discuss which backlog items were being picked in the next sprint.

Interviewee 66: "[…] they got some extra backlog items which are more important so they can't deliver, at least the decommitment is coming a little late and that is forcing us to not release our software […]."

The regular synchronization meeting brought about transparency on the status of backlog items and what the teams were currently working on. As the main focus was on communicating what backlog items were definitely going to be implemented in the coming sprint, the condition of predictability was established.

Beta-P2 Work Item Spanning Across Teams
In process *Beta-P2*, the absence of common understanding and accountability was recognized through a work item spanning across teams (see Fig. 4.12). This cross-team item was brought into the CPO/PO round for discussion and then

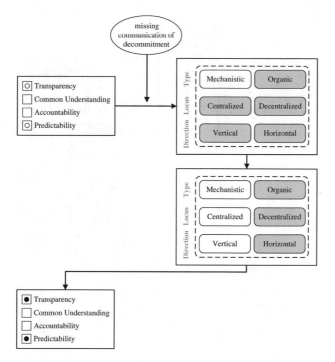

Fig. 4.11 Beta-P1 process

assigned to a leading PO. Interviewee 35 further described that as a leading PO for a backlog item it was now his responsibility to get into contact with the other team needed for this item and discuss how to proceed with the implementation. Time horizons were elaborated and possible blocking topics were eliminated. The decision of the two POs was then communicated back to the CPOs.

Interviewee 35: "I discuss with the other Product Owner and Scrum Master and ask if they can help and what to do. At the ground level, we get some kind of agreement and then we tell the CPO which topics are dropped from this team because this topic is more important and this team has to help here."

Through the intensive discussions among the team POs and SMs, the integrating conditions common understanding and accountability could be established.

Beta-P3 Unclear Usage of New Development Framework
The process *Beta-P3* (see Fig. 4.13), shows how a lack of common understanding became evident, because the usage of a new development framework was unclear to one development team. The CPOs had decided that a framework developed by another team was to be used by all other teams in the multiteam system. However, it was still unclear how to exactly use this framework and what the standards of usage were. To clarify these issues, additional information had to be acquired from the team that had developed it in order to properly use the framework.

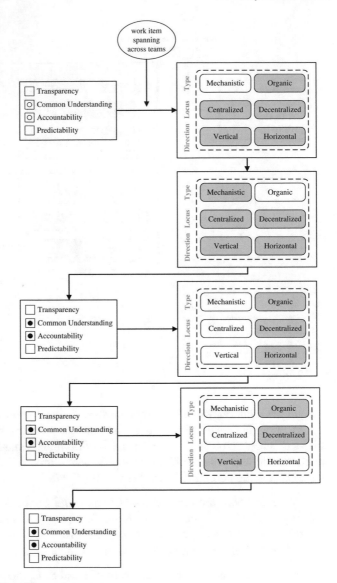

Fig. 4.12 Beta-P2 process

The direct exchange between the two teams led to a transfer of knowledge and a better awareness of how to use the framework. Because of this, a common understanding between these teams was established and supported the usage of the framework in the future.

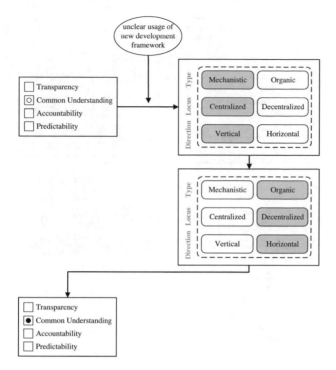

Fig. 4.13 Beta-P3 process

Beta-P4 Major Testing Failures of New Feature
In this process, the absence of the integrating condition common understanding became prevalent through major testing failures after a new feature was implemented (see Fig. 4.14). This feature required the contribution of several teams and it was not until the testing began that major failures started to show up. It became clear that the concept for this new feature was not reviewed with enough detail before the start of the implementation. The CPO level was immediately informed and got involved in the discussions among the teams. The CPO/PO round decided that patches were needed to fix the implemented functionality and encouraged the teams to deliver them quickly in order to solve the issues.

Through the discussion among all persons involved, a common understanding of the problems and how this situation arose was formed. Predictability was created by the encouragement of the CPO/PO round to deliver patches fast.

Beta-P5 New Cross Team Feature Originating From Team
The process *Beta-P5* (see Fig. 4.15) shows the establishment of three integrating conditions whose lack was noticed through the need to implement a new cross-team feature. This feature originated from one of the development teams and was discussed in the CPO/PO round and reviewed in the architecture round. After being discussed in both rounds, the feature was prepared enough to be rolled out via the

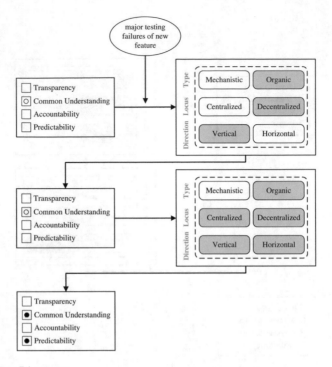

Fig. 4.14 Beta-P4 process

implementation plan originating from the CPO/PO round. After these steps, the lead team PO took over the coordination between the teams and this feature was implemented.

Common understanding was established through the discussions in the CPO/PO rounds together with the detailed review in the architecture meeting. The integrating condition accountability was created in the CPO/PO round via the implementation plan. Finally, predictability was gained through the implementation plan and the coordination of the lead PO.

Beta-P6 Priority Conflict Within Takt
Beta-P6 (see Fig. 4.16) illustrates a change in the coordination configuration due to a lack of common understanding, which was revealed by a priority conflict within the development takt. An interviewee reported of a situation, where in the middle of the development phase, a priority mismatch between two teams was discovered, which led to a problem in a completed task in one of the backlogs. This issue was immediately discussed among the team POs and a solution was found. The proposed solution was communicated to the CPOs via a change request, who accepted the resolution and communicated it to the rest of the POs in the multiteam system. This change request process had been institutionalized as this situation had occurred from time to time in the past. A common understanding between the teams was

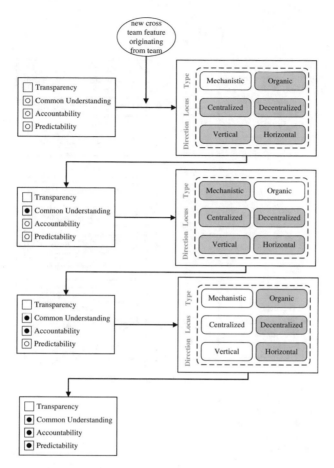

Fig. 4.15 Beta-P5 process

established through the discussions between the team POs. Accountability and predictability was created with the communication to the CPOs and their passing on of this information.

Beta-P7 Assumptions Mismatch

In process *Beta-P7* (see Fig. 4.17), the lack of common understanding was recognized because assumptions made during the time it was planned were not correct anymore. A topic which had been planned three iterations earlier was started in one team and began to face problems. It quickly became clear that assumptions made during the planning of this topic were not correct anymore and the topic needed to be stopped. The issues were discussed with the CPO level and the team decided that a topic rework was the best course of action.

Through the discussions with the CPO level, a common understanding of the topic was generated and a new approach could be taken.

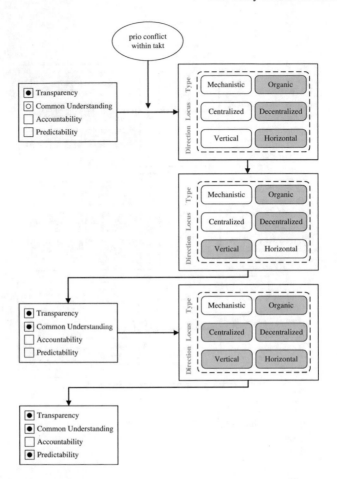

Fig. 4.16 Beta-P6 process

4.1.3 Case Gamma

The multiteam system *Gamma* was developing a mobile application development platform with seven teams in six main locations (see Table 4.5). The product in its current form had been under development for more than one year, but had existed in different forms previously. Many different technologies were used to implement the separate modules of this solution and thus the product complexity was rated as medium-high. The uncertainty of requirements was seen as low-medium as requirements did not appear to change much during the development phase.

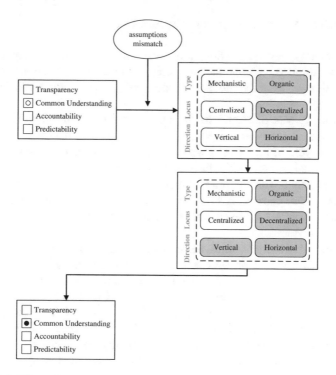

Fig. 4.17 Beta-P7 process

Table 4.5 Case gamma characteristics	Teams	7
	Locations	6
	Employees	~50
	Product type	On-premise and cloud
	Avg. Company Tenure	12 years
	Avg. MTS Tenure	5 years
	Avg. Team Tenure	3 years
	Avg. Role Tenure	2 years
	Product maturity	>1 year
	Customer delivery	4 months
	Team sprint length	2 weeks
	Product complexity	Medium-high
	Requirements uncertainty	Medium-high
	Inter-team coordination responsibility	SM

4.1.3.1   MTS Structure, Dependencies and Coordination

Due to its history, several previous products were integrated to compile this solution, which exhibited a compound structure. The teams were arranged according to the technical modules of the product and were solely responsible for their respective areas within the solution.

This product was delivered to the customer on a four monthly basis, with high-level release planning covering three months. The upcoming sprints were planned in a cycle of four weeks with individual sprints lasting two weeks.

The individual teams could influence the backlog in the beginning of the release through discussions with the product management. This influence dwindled as the development phase carried on, because backlog items were gradually more defined by a central architecture team and the release backlog could not be adapted anymore.

Unlike the previous two cases, the usage of a common backlog tool was clearly specified together with a process how to enter backlog items. The way in which these backlog items were broken down into user stories for the teams was centrally specified as well. In contrast to the first two MTSs, an overarching central information repository, e.g. in the form of a wiki, was not used. However, individual groups within this MTS had started to create such repositories to keep track of the accumulated knowledge in their fields (e.g. quality engineering). Awareness of other teams and the technology expertise was only passed on informally and mostly through verbal interaction with colleagues.

The inter-team dependencies depicted in Fig. 4.18 show a few two-way sequential dependencies between the core teams (Gamma 1-3). The other teams worked on very distinct modules, which did not need as much interaction, i.e. deliveries from the other teams. The number of strongly connected components in comparison to the number of teams also reinforces these distinct modules (see Table 4.6).

The general coordination style was described as a mix of top-down and bottom-up. Top-down coordination was evident in the time-frame, e.g. the shipment date, for current and future release as this was decided from management. The initial scope of the release in the form of high-level epics, was the responsibility of the product management but was the result of discussions with all participants, e.g. from individual teams and customers. These were detailed out by the central architecture team, which built prototypes and discussed with team architects on how to build the epics. The details of the user stories were worked out in collaboration between the central architecture team and the respective teams. However, the prioritization was decided solely by the product management. The bottom-up aspect of coordination was evident in the coordination between teams in the development sprints. It was the sole responsibility of the teams to communicate and synchronize with the other involved teams.

The problem solving strategy employed within Gamma relied heavily on a bottom-up approach, in that Scrum Masters and individual team roles discussed problems among their peers to come to a solution. These either surfaced in the

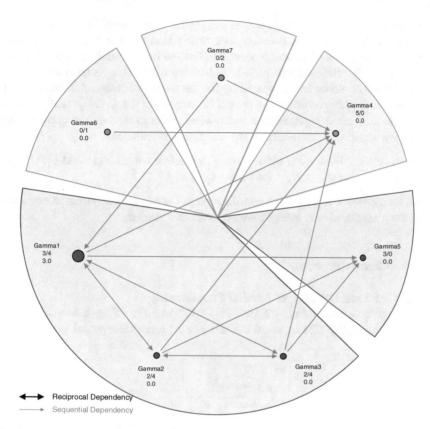

Fig. 4.18 Gamma inter-team task dependencies

Table 4.6 Case gamma
graph parameters

Graph parameter	Value
# Strongly connected components	5
Average degree	2.143
Density	0.357
Diameter	2

regular Scrum of Scrums call or were brought up and clarified in an ad hoc manner
between the individual teams.

4.1.3.2 Agile Method Scaling Approach

Scaling via Central Team Planning based on Team Inputs
In case Gamma, the scaling of coordination was done through a balance of central
planning and decentralized input from the development teams. The initial high-level
backlog items were gathered through input from the teams and the product

management. These were then detailed out by the central architecture team, which discussed technical and functional aspects with the individual development teams. Prototypes and proof of concepts were constructed in close collaboration with the teams. After this validation, the high-level backlog items were detailed out into user stories, which could be implemented by the development teams. All dependencies between teams were recorded in a central document. In the development phase, all Scrum Masters came together in a twice-weekly call to discuss the current status and review dependencies based on the mentioned document.

Interviewee 59: "We have a twice-weekly call where we discuss what is the status and what it is that the other teams are requesting."

All interviewees regarded the coordination in the multiteam system as good with some even mentioning it being a well-coordinated project.

4.1.3.3   Change Processes

Gamma-P1 Late Delivery of Needed Functionality
The change process *Gamma-P1* (see Fig. 4.19) was set off by a late delivery of needed functionality that exposed the absence of transparency and predictability.

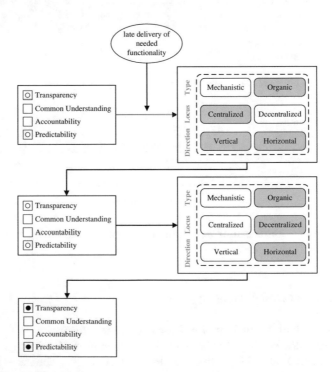

Fig. 4.19 Gamma-P1 process

One development team received a delivery from another team towards the end of the release cycle and still had to test the module. However, the late delivery did not allow for any fixes, in case errors were reported during testing. This situation was escalated to the Area Product Owner level, which decided to implement a twice-weekly call between teams to discuss such concerns.

Interviewee 59: "Such issues are now mitigated by having these calls, where we say 'ok this is the drop [of software functionality delivery] that we expect in this sprint.' We can negotiate about that and tell the requesting team why we need this drop earlier, because we are waiting for an integration test. This is one scenario that occurred because we get drops really late and then things get messed up in the end of the delivery cycle."

The integrating conditions transparency and predictability were created through this regular call, because the involved teams shared information on their status and thus allowed the other teams to judge deliveries.

Gamma-P2 Rapid Delivery of Patch Necessary
In process *Gamma-P2* (see Fig. 4.20), through the need for a rapid delivery of a patch, a deficiency in all integrating conditions became evident.

Interviewee 60: "We had to get a patch out very quickly. So we had sort of one person driving the coordination and what they did is, they listed out all the steps needed with everybody involved that needed to do something, [...] and the schedule was built right then and there and everybody had input into it and then people would just follow and [...] we delivered the patch in one day. And that is because everybody was saying 'I am done' and people kept checking in on each other and I think it went really well, because we were in constant communication."

Through the strong collaboration in the planning meeting, common understanding and accountability was established straight from the beginning. The intense communication and permanent status messages helped create transparency and predictability through up to date information on the progress.

Gamma-P3 Work Item Spanning Several Teams
The process *Gamma-P3* (see Fig. 4.21) depicts the absence of common understanding, accountability and predictability, which became evident through a work item spanning across several teams. The topic concept was worked out jointly in an initial conference call and was iteratively refined through follow-up conversations to clarify responsibilities and topic understanding. The decisions taken were then implemented in the iteration plan and the coordination was subsequently carried out between the involved team POs.

Interviewee 23: "We had an initial conference call, where we defined the topic [...] and then iteratively detailed out a plan which we were all satisfied with and then we started with the implementation."

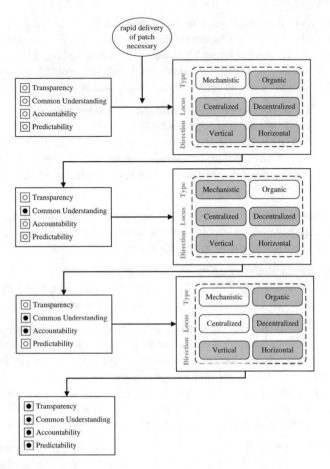

Fig. 4.20 Gamma-P2 process

Common understanding was created through the initial conference call and then refined through the iterative detailing of the topic. Within the collaboratively created iteration plan accountability and predictability was developed.

4.1.4 Case Delta

The next MTS, *Delta*, was developing a material management solution with six teams and around 85 employees (see Table 4.7). This multiteam system was entirely co-located and had been developing this solution for more than three years. Due to the integration of two comprehensive business areas with profound business domain knowledge necessary to grasp the processes contained in the solution, the

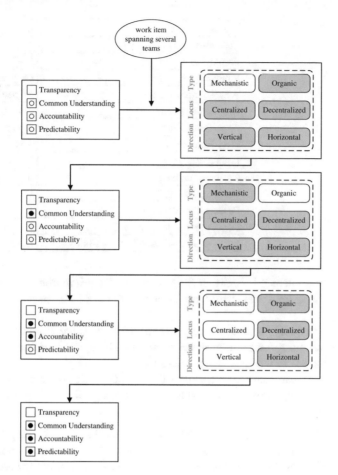

Fig. 4.21 Gamma-P3 process

product complexity was viewed as high. High-level requirements were detailed out in close collaboration with initial customers, who were generally aware of what they needed. The customers could supply long lists of what the solution should be able to provide and support, which is why the requirements uncertainty was rated low-medium. The product was developed as an on-premise solution that was characterized as an integrated system, modularized along the business process, which it supported.

4.1.4.1   MTS Structure, Dependencies and Coordination

As discussed above, the product integrated two very distinct business domains. Because of this, the teams either belonged to one of the business domains or

Table 4.7 Case delta
characteristics

Teams	6
Locations	1
Employees	~85
Product type	On-premise
Avg. Company Tenure	18 years
Avg. MTS Tenure	2 years
Avg. Team Tenure	3 years
Avg. Role Tenure	4 years
Product maturity	>3 years
Customer delivery	3 months
Team sprint length	4 weeks
Product complexity	High
Requirements uncertainty	Low-medium
Inter-team coordination responsibility	CPO, PO

fulfilled an integrative role between the two fields. Therefore, the team division in this multiteam system was based on business topics of the product they were developing.

Customer delivery of the product occurred every three months. The same time-frame was used for the high-level planning. The sprint length as well as the sprint planning cycle was both four weeks long.

The aspect of team autonomy was prevalent as POs were counted on to influence the product backlog. However, the adherence to certain rules and conventions was also expected.

Interviewer: "Can individual team POs influence the Product Backlog?"
Interviewee 12: "They are supposed to! If they do not, then in my opinion, they do not deserve the title Product Owner. If they want to have it finely sorted bit by bit from some higher authority, then they are demoted to assembly line workers and that cannot and should not be the case."
Interviewee 18: "Concerning certain topics we are relatively autonomous. But we are expected to adhere to certain things and be visible to the outside in a certain way. For example, we present our team backlog regularly and it is expected that it is prepared in a specific way."

The product management team had specified the usage of a common backlog tool and with it a clear process was implemented how backlog items were to be entered and then broken down into user stories for the teams. A comprehensive wiki was cultivated and maintained by all members of the MTS, including current information on the general setup of the multiteam system and material on technical and administrative aspects.

The inter-team dependencies in Fig. 4.22 show many one-way sequential dependencies. This is in line with the description of the interview partners that the

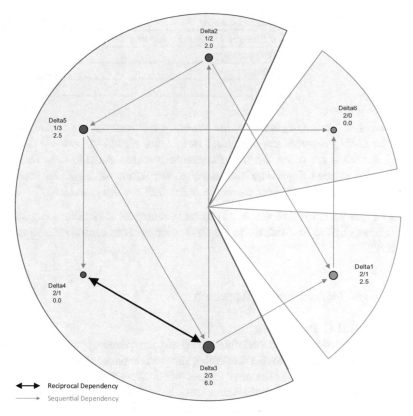

Fig. 4.22 Delta intra-team task dependencies

teams exhibited mainly producer-consumer relationships, in that functional deliveries were the cause of most interdependencies. The strongly connected components and the average degree values (see Table 4.8) underpin these sequential dependencies. The four teams grouped into one strongly connected component and the overall small number of dependencies to other teams (average degree) are as expected if one thinks of sequential linear dependencies between teams where one team delivers one process step of an overall business process.

The general coordination style in this multiteam system is best described as a mixed approach. On the one hand, it shows aspects of top-down in that the CPO determined many high level topics, but on the other hand also expected the team POs to actively engage in the development of the product backlog. What sets this multiteam system apart from the others is how they planned the next development iteration. At the beginning of each release, a planning workshop was conducted with all development teams to jointly plan the upcoming release. An entire day was scheduled for a workshop where all members of the MTS gathered in one room. The contents of this day are best described by one of the interviewees:

Table 4.8 Case delta graph parameters

Graph parameter	Value
# Strongly connected components	3
Average degree	1.667
Density	0.333
Diameter	3

Interviewee 13: "At the beginning of the release, we introduced the backlog to each other. The CPO presented the high-level view, what should the release deliver in the end, the business value, what is the customer value etc. Then the individual team POs introduced their backlogs and then the teams discussed dependencies and broke it all down into user stories in individual breakout sessions."

Despite this collaborative nature of planning, unexpected situations or problems between teams had to be escalated to the CPO or other more central roles in order to be resolved.

4.1.4.2   Agile Method Scaling Approach

Scaling via Full Collaboration

The multiteam system Delta had introduced a joint planning workshop several releases ago. In the run-up to this workshop, the team Product Owners prepared the high-level backlog items for the next release, which were to be discussed that day. On the workshop day itself, all the teams were introduced to the business cases for the next release of the software product by the CPO and then started with individual sessions to break down their team backlogs. Dependencies to other teams or topics, which were still unclear, could be discussed right away with the appropriate people. Overall, the employees in the MTS were very pleased with this approach.

Interviewee 13: "This is evolving very well. I'm very satisfied!"

Contrary to this very inclusive and involving approach for release planning, the problem solving strategy within this case still relied on escalation to the CPO.

4.1.4.3   Change Processes

Delta-P1 Competing Concept Deadlock

Process *Delta-P1* (see Fig. 4.23) pictures a competing concept deadlock situation. This deadlock situation exposed a lack of accountability, as two teams were proposing different suggestions that had the other team respectively doing more work. The Product Owner of one team came up with a concept for one of the requirements, which involved only small changes in this team but larger implementation tasks in another team. The PO of this other team suggested a different

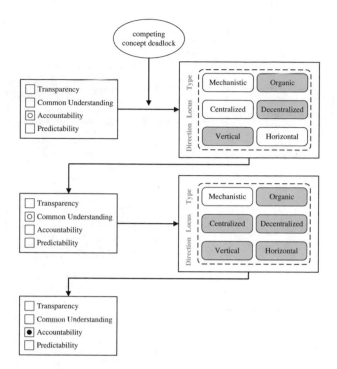

Fig. 4.23 Delta-P1 process

approach, which essentially reversed the effort. No agreement could be made between the two teams about how to proceed. This situation was escalated to the CPO who then got involved in the discussions. As this was a very technical issue, he involved a trusted advisor and decided how to solve this implementation question.

Interviewee 12: "PO1 says, 'ok if I do this in my team, this small piece, then it should work. How about you do the rest?' PO2 says, 'hmm, if we implement it the other way around, then we only have to do a small part which I believe is manageable, then your team can do the rest.' A deadlock situation, which has to be so resolved somehow."

The missing condition accountability was established through the intervention of the CPO and his decision about which of the concepts to implement.

Delta-P2 Unresolved Prioritization of Topic
This process shows the change process of the coordination configuration due to a lack of accountability and predictability, which became evident in the form of an unresolved prioritization of a topic (see Fig. 4.24). This topic was left for the teams to resolve and stagnated over the course of a few weeks. The CPO learned about this situation and intervened. They assigned a high priority to the backlog item as

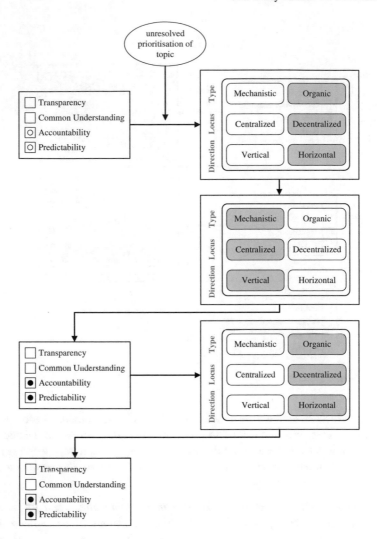

Fig. 4.24 Delta-P2 process

well as an accountable PO. Through this decision, the CPO created accountability and predictability and allowed the coordination between the teams to proceed as well as the implementation of the requirement to continue.

Interviewee 20: "Before, it plodded along, it was not aligned, not prioritized. After the decision, it had a clear priority, a high priority. It was implemented then accordingly. From my perspective, it worked because it was sufficiently prioritized and it was clearly said who was in charge."

Delta-P3 Cross-Team Item Facing Asymmetric Team Knowledge

The process *Delta-P3* (see Fig. 4.25) shows a lack of common understanding with transparency and accountability already present at the time of the trigger. A work item spanning across two teams led to the situation that one team did not have enough knowledge concerning the requirement in order to implement it. It was decided between the two teams that a knowledge exchange was needed. The team with the expertise shared this knowledge through information sessions and thus ensured a smooth development. This process differs from the other presented processes here, as no coordination configuration change happened. However, due to the already strong presence of transparency and accountability at the time of the trigger, the lack of common understanding did not necessitate a change in the configuration. The condition common understanding was established through the intensification of the already present organic and decentralized configuration between the teams in order to overcome the lack of common understanding.

4.1.5 Case Epsilon

The last multiteam system presented here was developing a solution to manage safety processes and their compliance. With around 40 employees in four teams at

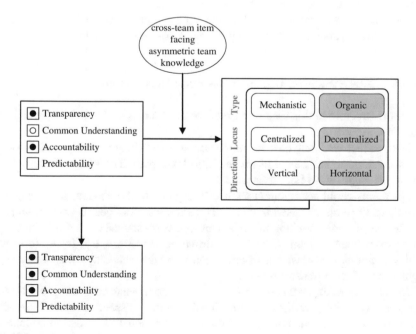

Fig. 4.25 Delta-P3 process

Table 4.9 Case epsilon characteristics

Teams	4
Locations	3
Employees	~40
Product type	On-premise and cloud
Avg. Company Tenure	13 years
Avg. MTS Tenure	7 years
Avg. Team Tenure	5 years
Avg. Role Tenure	3 years
Product maturity	>10 years
Customer delivery	3 months
Team sprint length	4 weeks
Product complexity	Medium-high
Requirements uncertainty	Medium-high
Inter-team coordination responsibility	PO, Architect

three locations, *Epsilon* was developing both an on-premise as well as a cloud version of their product (see Table 4.9). Due to the integration of four distinctive components in this solution, the product complexity was seen as medium-high. Requirements uncertainty was also viewed as medium-high due to the changing nature of regulatory compliance standards and the close collaboration with customers wishing to adapt the product to their needs.

The solution was made up of four separate modules, which had little overlap from a content perspective but which shared a common technological foundation.

4.1.5.1   MTS Structure, Dependencies and Coordination

The team structure in this case was based on the four separate modules, which this solution combined.

The product was delivered to the customer approximately every three months. The same time-frame was used for the high-level plan. The sprint planning cycle and sprint length were both four weeks.

The teams could act autonomously with regards to the content, but technology wise there were clear standards which the teams were obliged to comply with.

The use of a joint backlog management tool was established, but its usage style varied from team to team. A central information repository, e.g. in the form of a wiki, was not used. Knowledge of other teams and the technology was passed on in regular information transfer sessions.

The inter-team dependencies in Fig. 4.26 are somewhat misleading, as the four teams had very little overlap and dependencies in their respective topics. What they did share was the foundation layer where teams Epsilon 1–3 needed to collaborate from time to time in order to implement new requirements. In line with this

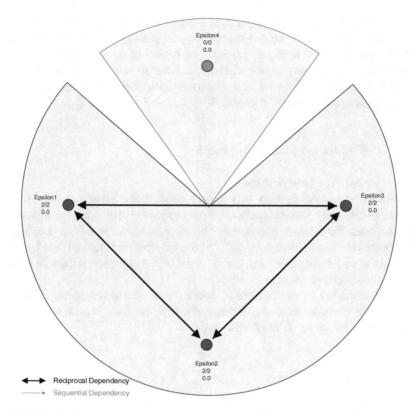

Fig. 4.26 Epsilon inter-team task dependencies

characterization, the graph parameters (see Table 4.10) are less meaningful as in the other cases.

The general coordination style of Epsilon can be summarized as bottom-up with top-down guidance. Regular input from customers to the team POs was discussed on an ad hoc basis with the CPO to decide if, when and how to implement these requests. The CPO in the end decided what was going to be implemented. The detailed implementation was then discussed with the customers by the POs.

The problem solving strategy of this MTS was built on communication between the team POs. If unexpected issues arose or problems needed to be solved, discussions among the teams were carried out for clarification. As the MTS exhibited little dependencies between teams and the topic of each team was also very distinct,

Table 4.10 Case epsilon graph parameters

Graph parameter	Value
# Strongly connected components	2
Average degree	1.500
Density	0.500
Diameter	1

more responsibility and autonomy lay in the hands of the team POs. If they were not able to clear up issues among themselves, an escalation path was given to the CPO who got involved in the discussion and helped in solving the matter.

Each team consistently practiced the sprint retrospective to review their own team and inter-team processes and improve upon them. Previous topics were tracked and inspected each retrospective.

4.1.5.2   Agile Method Scaling Approach

Scaling via Ad Hoc Communication
Since the teams in case Epsilon only shared a foundation layer and the rest of the implementation work was independent from each other, the need for task coordination between the teams was reduced. Therefore, the weekly CPO/PO call served as an update meeting to inform the CPO of the status of each team. If the teams had to extend the underlying platform, the involved teams communicated selectively to implement the needed features.

The coordination in the multiteam system was considered to be quite good, because an open communication culture allowed the easy access of other team members if a feature required outside input.

4.1.5.3   Change Processes

Epsilon-P1 Recognition of Reuse Possibility
Similar to process Delta-P3, *Epsilon-P1* (see Fig. 4.27) shows no change in the coordination configuration. One team presented a new topic to another team to find

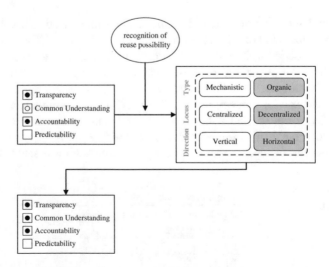

Fig. 4.27 Epsilon-P1 process

out if this would be of benefit to them as well. A reuse possibility was recognized and so the two team POs discussed possibilities how to adapt the topic.

The reason behind this lack of change is the same as in the previous process; the already strong presence of two integrating conditions only needed the intensification in the already enacted configuration to attain common understanding between the teams.

Epsilon-P2 Discovery of Redundancies

In process *Epsilon-P2* (see Fig. 4.28), the lack of three integrating conditions was exposed by the discovery of redundancies. In the backlogs of two teams, duplicate work was encountered and both teams had the understanding that the other team would implement this item and nothing happened. After a while, the team POs discussed with the CPO how to mitigate such problems in the future. The decision to increase the frequency of synchronization meetings between those teams was taken.

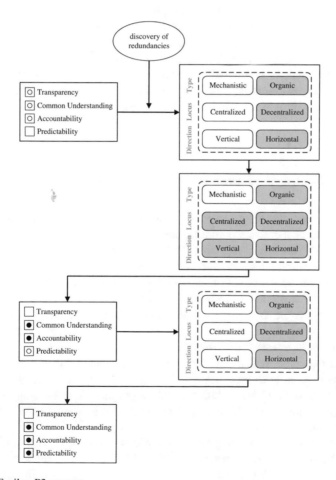

Fig. 4.28 Epsilon-P2 process

Interviewee 26: "So, there was somehow missing coordination and not enough communication, that one of the teams was with the understanding that the other team will take care of the topic. So after one or two months it appeared that this was not the case."

Through this increase and the exchange of information between the teams, transparency as well as common understanding was established. The creation of accountability was due to the introduced regular meeting which also involved discussions on the responsibility of each backlog item.

4.2 Cross-Case Analysis

After providing a very detailed picture of each studied MTS, what follows is a cross-case analysis of those aspects that pose questions as to how and why they differ across the examined cases. Imbalances of integrating conditions are presented first, followed by the specific instantiations of coordination configurations investigated in this research and their description. An analysis of the relationship between coordination configurations and integrating conditions as well as an analysis of the coordination configuration dimensions proceeds afterwards. The chapter closes with a temporal analysis of integrating conditions and coordination configurations.

4.2.1 Imbalances of Integrating Conditions

The depicted processes in the previous chapter show clearly that a change process was initiated once a deficiency of integrating conditions for coordinated action was recognized. All processes were provoked by the absence of one or several of the integrating conditions. However, the participants of the coordination process were seldom aware of the underlying factors that were missing. A triggering event acted as the catalyst for the actors to become aware of their absence. These triggering events can either be of a regular deliberate nature (e.g. Fig. 4.15) or happen abruptly and constitute a deviation (e.g. Fig. 4.3) from everyday business. The regular deliberate events imply that this type of event was foreseen or the unexpected was expected in that deviations from a plan were anticipated. The abrupt events constitute an unforeseen issue, which did not have any resolving process in place and needed an ad hoc solution to allow progress. Interestingly, these unexpected triggers happened with a surprising regularity in some of the studied multiteam systems.

When focusing on the integrating conditions across all cases studied, three questions are of particular interest (see Table 4.11). The first being how many times which integrating condition was missing at the onset of a particular coordination

Table 4.11 Descriptive values integrating conditions

		Transparency	Common understanding	Accountability	Predictability
Sum of missing integrating conditions	Alpha	3	5	3	2
	Beta	1	6	2	2
	Gamma	2	2	2	3
	Delta	0	1	2	1
	Epsilon	1	2	1	0
	Total	7	16	10	8
Unachieved integrating conditions	Alpha	3	3	1	1
	Beta	0	0	0	0
	Gamma	0	0	0	0
	Delta	–	0	0	0
	Epsilon	0	0	0	–
Additionally established integrating conditions	Alpha	0	0	2	2
	Beta	0	0	0	2
	Gamma	0	0	0	0
	Delta	0	0	0	0
	Epsilon	0	0	0	0

process (row one in Table 4.11). The second question concerns itself with the amount of unachieved integrating conditions (row two in Table 4.11). Here, the number of instances where a certain integrating condition was identified as being lacking in the beginning of the coordination process and this still being the case at the end of this process is of interest. The final question is what additional integrating conditions were established which were not lacking at the onset of the coordination process (row three in Table 4.11).

The sum of missing integrating conditions (row one in Table 4.11) displays common understanding as the top condition missing in the investigated coordination processes. It seems that one of the main problems within MTS is achieving a shared understanding of the mostly complex topics processed. The three other integrating conditions achieve similar values across all cases. The unachieved integrating conditions (row two in Table 4.11) shows values skewed towards transparency and common understanding. In the investigated processes, these two conditions seem to be harder to attain. As accountability and predictability can be attained relatively easily by intervention from outside or from higher up the hierarchy, it seems plausible that these would be achieved more often. In the case of transparency, the teams themselves must provide information, which can be drowned out in the day-to-day work or if more pressing issues are at the forefront of attention. Common understanding, finally, necessitates at least two actors, which have to be willing to absorb information and be able to understand what someone else is trying to convey. In comparison, this appears to be much harder to achieve.

In the cases under study, only Alpha showed these unachieved integrating conditions in the coordination processes examined.

Additionally established integrating conditions (row three in Table 4.11) could be seen in cases Alpha and Beta. Here, accountability and predictability were created although not initially needed in the coordination process. In the two instances of accountability creation, this can be viewed as an alternative to the initial lack of common understanding (processes Alpha-P1 and Alpha-P2). The two teams could have solved their coordination problem, i.e. who is responsible for what by having a common understanding of the current activities. This not being the case, the central team had to step in, assign accountable teams, and thereby solve this coordination problem.

In order to investigate potential relations between the integrating conditions, Table 4.12 shows the number of integrating conditions which were found to be lacking together with other integrating conditions. The cells which have the same integrating condition in the row as well as the column show instances where solely this particular integrating condition was lacking. In case Alpha, transparency was often lacking at the same time that common understanding was missing as well. This case shows two instances where a single integrating condition was lacking in a coordination process, namely common understanding and accountability. Case Beta shows three occurrences where only common understanding was lacking. Furthermore, accountability and common understanding appeared to be lacking together in two instances.

Overall, common understanding and accountability as well as accountability and predictability appeared to be lacking together in six instances. The lack of common understanding and accountability seems intuitive, as both aspects are at the heart of productive collaboration between teams. On the one hand, everybody involved needs to have an understanding of the topic in development and on the other, it needs to be decided who is doing what in order to develop software in a timely fashion. Transparency and common understanding as well as common understanding and predictability were lacking together in five occurrences across all cases and processes investigated. Only two of the integrating conditions appeared to be lacking singularly. Common understanding and accountability were lacking alone in four and two processes respectively.

4.2.2   Deriving Instantiations of Coordination Configurations

In order to examine the source of each final integrating condition, all processes were scrutinized and the originating coordination configuration was recorded for each final integrating condition for each process (see Appendix E Process Overview). To achieve a better overview of all processes, a miniature representation of the coordination configuration was chosen as depicted in Fig. 4.29.

Table 4.12 Lack of integrating conditions appearing together

Alpha	Transparency	Common Understanding	Accountability	Predictability	Beta	Transparency	Common Understanding	Accountability	Predictability
Transparency	0	3	1	1		0	0	0	1
Common Understanding		1	2	2			3	2	1
Accountability			1	2				0	1
Predictability				0					0
Gamma					**Delta**				
Transparency	0	1	1	2		0	0	0	0
Common Understanding		0	2	2			0	0	0
Accountability			0	2				1	1
Predictability				0					0
Epsilon					**All**				
Transparency	0	1	1	0		0	5	3	4
Common Understanding		0	0	0			4	6	5
Accountability			0	0				2	6
Predictability				0					0

Fig. 4.29 Miniature
representation of the
coordination configuration

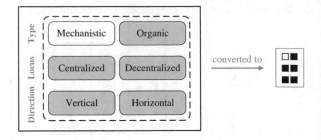

Fig. 4.30 Coordination
configurations leading to
integrating conditions

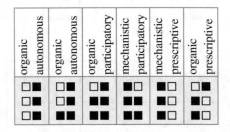

In the 22 processes investigated, only a limited number of coordination configurations lead to the creation of integrating conditions. Overall, six configurations led to the establishment of integrating conditions in the presented processes (see Fig. 4.30). These six configurations can be grouped according to the type of coordination mechanism employed, which is either mechanistic or organic. The second dimension is the degree of co-management present in the respective configuration. The three aspects are autonomous, participatory and prescriptive. The autonomous aspect implies that the team could coordinate in an independent fashion without being subject to other entities within the MTS. The participatory aspect describes a coordination configuration in which central actors in the MTS (e.g. CPO or central teams) and the development teams consider themselves as equals and jointly come to decisions based on mutual discussion for example. On the opposite side of this spectrum lies the prescriptive aspect, where central actors impose decisions on development teams and team POs without their participation in the decision process.

The first two configurations under the heading *organic autonomous configuration* are characterized by an organic coordination mechanism, decentralized locus and a horizontal or both horizontal and vertical direction. An example of this configuration would be a direct team-to-team communication in the form of an informal chat between team Product Owners. If the results of this chat were communicated to the CPO, the vertical direction would also be highlighted in the configuration.

The next two configurations both exhibit a participatory nature, in that both central and decentral entities participate in the coordination and the direction is horizontal as well as vertical. They differ in the mechanism they enact, one shows mechanistic, the other organic mechanisms. A meeting with team Product Owners and Chief Product Owners, where the participants collaboratively discuss issues, would be an example of an *organic participatory configuration*. If in said meeting a plan was collaboratively created, then this would be a *mechanistic participatory configuration*.

The last two of the five configurations are based on a centralized locus with a vertical direction and either a mechanistic or an organic mechanism. An example of a *mechanistic prescriptive configuration* is a plan developed by a central team, which is then pushed into the development teams. The *organic* variation could be a decision by a CPO that is then verbally communicated to others.

4.2.3 Analysis of the Relationship Between Integrating Conditions and Coordination Configurations

Transparency. In all cases where transparency was established in one of the change processes, it was created in an organic autonomous configuration (see Fig. 4.31). Recalling the definition of transparency from Sect. 4.1.1.1, "the perceived quality of intentionally shared information from a sender" (Schnackenberg and Tomlinson 2014, p. 5), this comes as no surprise. As the information needs to be "intentionally shared" from one team with the rest of the MTS, this happens predominantly in autonomous configurations as only the teams themselves can choose to provide such information. While one could imagine a more centralized approach with central provisions on information sharing, the teams could avoid these simply by not letting anyone know about certain aspects happening within the team. Furthermore, as the coordination between teams was of interest and many of the investigated processes were the result of an unexpected trigger, the easiest, and perhaps fastest, way to achieve this condition is by organically coordinating, e.g. communicating directly with another team. It follows, at least with respect to the five cases examined here, that transparency is only generated from within the team in an autonomous fashion.

Common Understanding. This integrating condition was generated in organic configurations across all five cases (see Fig. 4.31). Based on the definition "a shared perspective on the whole task and how individuals' work fits within the whole" (Okhuysen and Bechky 2009, p. 488), it seems that this shared perspective is best created through organic communication among the participants in the MTS. The central aspect within the organic mechanism is the focus on communication as a means for coordination. While a mechanistic coordination (i.e. a plan) could impart some form of common understanding among the participants of the coordination process, it is always limited by its rigidity and one-way information transfer. It is the goal of mechanistic coordination to limit communication and thus ensure efficiency. Precisely this reason makes it difficult to exchange information of a complex nature. Communication in the form of verbal exchange on the other hand offers

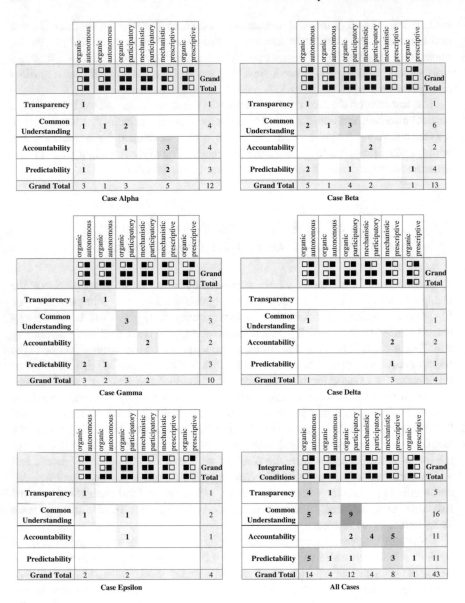

Fig. 4.31 Coordination configurations leading to integrating conditions across all cases

the possibility to collaboratively come to an understanding of the topic at hand. Furthermore, in this two-way communication, the involved entities can ensure that a *common understanding* is present and not only an information transfer with imperfect understanding. As such, organic coordination can be viewed as the foundation for understanding and building a common mental model for complex topics.

The originating configurations of this integrating condition can be distinguished between ones which are of a pure bottom-up nature (e.g. organic, decentralized and horizontal) and ones in which central involvement is discernible. As such, the MTSs created a common understanding mostly in a decentral manner between the involved teams (see Case Delta Fig. 4.31) or in a participatory manner where more central actors of the MTS took part as well, without prescribing what to do (see Case Gamma Fig. 4.31).

These first two integrating conditions could be linked to originating coordination configurations rather clearly. The conditions accountability and predictability paint a more diffuse picture. Both of these integrating conditions could not be clearly associated with individual configurations across all cases, rather it seems that there are different ways in how to create these two integrating conditions.

Accountability. Accountability "addresses the question of who is responsible for specific elements of the task and makes clear where the responsibilities of interdependent parties lie" (Okhuysen and Bechky 2009, p. 483). In the five cases investigated, accountability was mostly created in mechanistic configurations, either in a prescriptive manner or through participation of all involved parties (see Fig. 4.31). The mechanistic coordination mechanisms, e.g. plans, rules or roles, inherently impart a form of accountability. A role assignment's goal is to identify and define a responsible person. Similarly, a plan will pinpoint what should be achieved and who should complete it—another form of accountability determination. The question of who is responsible is usually established through role definitions or captured through the creation of a plan in the form of assignees in the backlog management tool, which exemplifies the mechanistic nature of these configurations. The two instances where accountability was established in an organic participatory configuration can be traced back to missing clarity between actors. As such, a misunderstanding concerning accountability is more easily clarified through communication and participation of all involved parties.

Cases Gamma and Beta exhibited mechanistic participatory configurations in order to establish accountability. Here, responsibility was assigned jointly in meetings with all parties involved or through self-assignment. In the cases Alpha and Delta, accountability was created through prescriptive action, in that work items were externally or centrally assigned to teams. The way in which these assignments come to be, e.g. through self-assignment or through external assignment, seems to be the central distinguishing element in the difference between the prescriptive and participatory nature of these two groups.

Predictability. Predictability "enables interdependent parties to anticipate subsequent task related activity by knowing what the elements of the task are and when they happen" (Okhuysen and Bechky 2009, p. 486). In the all cases chart of Fig. 4.31, the creation of predictability was rather dispersed across all coordination configurations. However, an accumulation can be seen in organic autonomous and mechanistic prescriptive configurations. Cases Beta and Gamma enacted organic autonomous configurations more often to establish predictability than other configurations. Through participatory involvement in planning and thus accountability, the teams considered their work items their own and felt responsible to ensure predictability to other teams and the program they were working in. The other identifiable group consists of cases Alpha and Delta, which predominantly created predictability in mechanistic prescriptive configurations. The prescriptive nature of planning and work item allocation in these two cases did not seem to create the same amount of identification with the work as in the other cases investigated. As such, predictability was established extrinsically through directives that prescribed a certain amount of reporting to the other or central teams.

4.2.4   Analysis of the Relationship Between the Coordination Configuration Dimensions and the Integrating Conditions

The previously established instantiations of the coordination configuration show two dimensions along which they can be grouped. The first one being the type of coordination mechanism employed, namely organic or mechanistic. The second one can be described as the degree of co-management present in the respective configuration. The three facets here are autonomous, participatory and prescriptive. The autonomous facet contains the notion of a sovereign coordination process independent of other actors within the multiteam system. The participatory facet describes a coordination in which an equal representation of more central actors and the development teams is achieved. An example are the joint discussion and decision meetings of CPOs and POs where important decisions are made on a mutual basis. Quite the contrary can be seen in the prescriptive configurations, where central actors, such as the CPO or a central team, take decisions which are then enforced throughout the MTS.

Figure 4.32 shows organic versus mechanistic mechanisms and which integrating conditions were established when employing each. The key question is, if the coordination mechanism employed is independent of the established integrating condition. The contingency table shown in Fig. 4.32 was used as the base for a chi-squared test of independence. The null hypothesis $H_0 = coordination\ configurations\ are\ independent\ of\ the\ integrating\ conditions$ was established with the alternative hypothesis being that the coordination configurations and the integrating conditions have an association. The results of Pearson's Chi-squared test show a p-value of 0.00002472. This leads us to the conclusion that the results are highly significant on a $p < 0.001$ level. Based on this the null hypothesis can be rejected.

However, sparsely populated contingency tables are a problem for Pearson's Chi-squared test of independence, in particular cells with an expected value of less than five lead to an incorrect approximation of the Chi-squared value (Hogg and Tanis 1996). To overcome this issue, another test can be employed. An approach for small contingency tables is Fisher's exact test, which, as the name implies, calculates exact p-values. In the test of independence of organic and mechanistic coordination configurations and the integrating conditions in which they were established, the exact test provides an even lower p-value ($p = 0.000005803 < 0.001$) and thus

Fig. 4.32 Analysis of organic versus mechanistic coordination configurations leading to integrating conditions

Integrating Conditions	organic	mechanistic	Grand Total
Transparency	5	0	5
Common Understanding	16	0	16
Accountability	2	9	11
Predictability	8	3	11
Grand Total	31	12	43

Pearson's Chi-squared test
$$\chi^2 = 24.022$$
$$df = 3$$
$$p\text{-value} = 0.00002472$$

Fisher's Exact Test for Count Data
p-value = 0.000005803

supports the result of the Chi-squared test. Therefore, highly significant support to reject the null hypothesis of independence of integrating conditions and coordination configurations in the form of organic or mechanistic configuration is given. Hence, it is highly likely that organic and mechanistic configurations are used to establish different integrating conditions.

Another way of merging the coordination configurations is by their autonomous, participatory or prescriptive nature. This can be seen in Fig. 4.33. The same tests of independence as previously mentioned were conducted on this contingency table. The results of Pearson's Chi-squared test show a p-value of 0.0004167. This leads us to the conclusion that the results are highly significant on a $p < 0.001$ level. Based on this, the null hypothesis of coordination configuration dimensions being independent of integrating conditions can be rejected. Fisher's exact test supports this statement with a p-value of 0.00003473.

4.2.5   Temporal Analysis of Integrating Conditions and Coordination Configurations

The following sections will dive into the temporal analysis of the investigated coordination processes. To begin with, the aspect of time is enfolded by detailing

Fig. 4.33 Analysis of
autonomous versus
participatory versus
prescriptive coordination
configurations leading to
integrating conditions

Integrating Conditions	autonomous	participatory	prescriptive	Grand Total
Transparency	5	0	0	5
Common Understanding	7	9	0	16
Accountability	0	6	5	11
Predictability	6	1	4	11
Grand Total	18	16	9	43

Pearson's Chi-squared test
$$\chi^2 = 24.532$$
$$df = 6$$
$$\text{p-value} = 0.0004167$$

Fisher's Exact Test for Count Data
p-value = 0.00003473

the process sequences from the point of view of all cases together as well as the five cases individually. Subsequently, the integrating conditions and their differing establishment across these process steps will be the focal point.

All Cases. The overall view across all cases in Fig. 4.36 shows the temporal sequence of integrating condition creation. The horizontal axis show the six instantiations of the coordination configurations, while the vertical axis shows the coordination process split up into the three process steps which were at most necessary. These process steps originate from the single case analysis where the individual processes depicted one to three change steps before being completed. The figures show the aggregated data per MTS/overall split up into the individual process steps. The data shows that common understanding was addressed strongly in the first step of the coordination process. In some instances accountability and in one instance predictability was focused on initially. Transparency was never attended to in the first process step across any of the cases. In the second step, all integrating conditions were established, with a strong focus on accountability and predictability. Here, transparency was first created in the coordination process. The third and final step shows no establishment of common understanding and little accountability creation. However, transparency and predictability are still created in this step.

Alpha. In case Alpha (see Fig. 4.34), the initial focus lay on accountability with single instances of common understanding and predictability creation present in the data. In the second step, common understanding was established in three configurations, with accountability and predictability being created twice each. Finally, transparency was produced once in this process step as well. Case Alpha only showed two process steps across all coordination processes observed.

Beta. The coordination processes in case Beta (see Fig. 4.34) exhibited a strong focus on common understanding creation in the first step, with no other integrating condition being established this early in the process. The second step shows generation of accountability twice, as well as one occurrence of transparency and predictability. Finally, the third and last process step displays another instance of transparency creation and a stronger focus on predictability with two occasions establishing this integrating condition.

Gamma. Similar to Beta, case Gamma (see Fig. 4.35) focused on early generation of common understanding. Step 2 shows the establishment of transparency and predictability and two instances of accountability creation. The third and final

Case Alpha

Step 1	organic autonomous	organic autonomous	organic autonomous	organic participatory	mechanistic participatory	mechanistic prescriptive	organic prescriptive	Grand Total
Transparency								
Common Understanding				1				1
Accountability						2		2
Predictability						1		1

Step 2								
Transparency	1							1
Common Understanding	1	1	1					3
Accountability					1	1		2
Predictability	1					1		2

Step 3								
Transparency								
Common Understanding								
Accountability								
Predictability								

Case Beta

Step 1	organic autonomous	organic autonomous	organic autonomous	organic participatory	mechanistic participatory	mechanistic prescriptive	organic prescriptive	Grand Total
Transparency								
Common Understanding				3				3
Accountability								
Predictability								

Step 2								
Transparency	1							1
Common Understanding								
Accountability						2		2
Predictability	1							1

Step 3								
Transparency		1						1
Common Understanding								
Accountability								
Predictability	1	1						2

Fig. 4.34 Coordination configurations leading to integrating conditions split into process steps for cases alpha and beta

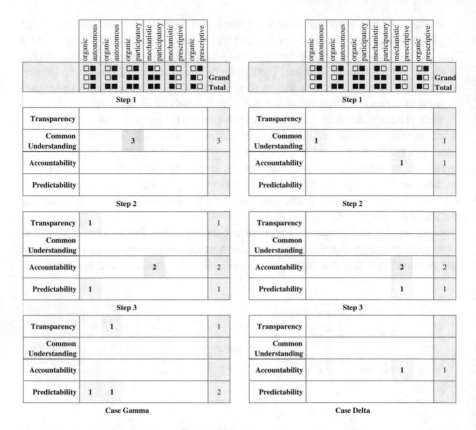

Fig. 4.35 Coordination configurations leading to integrating conditions split into process steps for cases gamma and delta

process step exhibits transparency establishment and two occurrences of predictability creation.

Delta. In the first step of the coordination processes within this case (see Fig. 4.35), common understanding and accountability were created in two instances. The second step exhibits two occurrences of accountability creation and one predictability establishment. In the final step, accountability was created in one coordination process.

Epsilon. The last case, shown in Fig. 4.36, exhibits common understanding establishment in process step 1. In the second step, case Epsilon created common understanding and accountability in one occurrence each. In the third and final process step, transparency was generated in one instance.

While the previous sections offered the temporal analysis from the point of view of the five cases investigated, the following sections will present the analysis from the perspective of the integrating condition.

Transparency. From a time perspective, transparency was created in later steps of the change process (see illustrations Figs. 4.34, 4.35 and 4.36). In none of the

Case Epsilon

Step 1

	organic autonomous	organic autonomous	organic participatory	mechanistic participatory	mechanistic prescriptive	organic prescriptive	Grand Total
Transparency							
Common Understanding	1						1
Accountability							
Predictability							

Step 2

	organic autonomous	organic autonomous	organic participatory	mechanistic participatory	mechanistic prescriptive	organic prescriptive	Grand Total
Transparency							
Common Understanding			1				1
Accountability			1				1
Predictability							

Step 3

	organic autonomous	organic autonomous	organic participatory	mechanistic participatory	mechanistic prescriptive	organic prescriptive	Grand Total
Transparency	1						1
Common Understanding							
Accountability							
Predictability							

All Cases

Step 1

	organic autonomous	organic autonomous	organic participatory	mechanistic participatory	mechanistic prescriptive	organic prescriptive	Grand Total
Transparency							0
Common Understanding	2		7				9
Accountability					3		3
Predictability					1		1

Step 2

	organic autonomous	organic autonomous	organic participatory	mechanistic participatory	mechanistic prescriptive	organic prescriptive	Grand Total
Transparency	3						3
Common Understanding	1	1	2				4
Accountability			2	4	3		9
Predictability	3				2		5

Step 3

	organic autonomous	organic autonomous	organic participatory	mechanistic participatory	mechanistic prescriptive	organic prescriptive	Grand Total
Transparency	1	2					3
Common Understanding							0
Accountability					1		1
Predictability	22						4

Fig. 4.36 Coordination configurations leading to integrating conditions split into process steps for case epsilon and all cases

cases was it established in the first step. It seems that the MTSs deemed the other integrating conditions such as common understanding and accountability to be more critical in early steps of coordination. Another line of explanation would be the argument, that for there to be transparency, the aspects of common understanding and accountability need to be in place first. In other words, first one needs to come to a common understanding of what is being development before one can intentionally share information about that development.

Common Understanding. This integrating condition was created early in the change process in cases Beta, Gamma, Delta and Epsilon. Only in case Alpha was this condition mostly generated in later process steps (see illustrations Figs. 4.34, 4.35 and 4.36). This could be explained by the fact that one usually has to first come to an understanding of what is being developed before transparency, accountability and predictability become more important. However, in case Alpha the central team allocated work items to teams and therefore established accountability before a common understanding was sought.

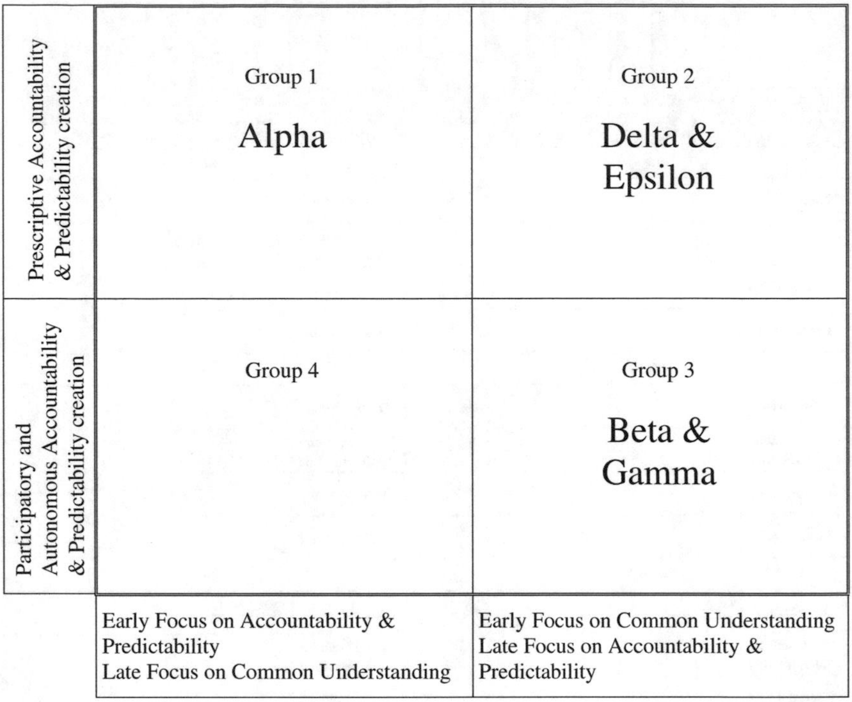

	Group 1 Alpha	Group 2 Delta & Epsilon
Prescriptive Accountability & Predictability creation		
Participatory and Autonomous Accountability & Predictability creation	Group 4	Group 3 Beta & Gamma
	Early Focus on Accountability & Predictability Late Focus on Common Understanding	Early Focus on Common Understanding Late Focus on Accountability & Predictability

Fig. 4.37 Three stereotypes of multiteam systems

Accountability and Predictability. These two integrating condition were established at two distinct points in time, depending on the case. Case Alpha stands out as creating these integrating conditions early on. Only in one instance did case Delta create accountability in the first process step. Cases Beta, Gamma, Delta and Epsilon established these two integrating conditions later in the coordination process. A possible explanation could be the already mentioned initial focus on creating a common understanding before decisions on accountability are taken. A later focus on predictability seems plausible as work needs to be done first before its status can be communicated to others.

In the analysis of the integrating conditions of coordination, an answer to the question of how these conditions were attained was sought. Previous literature that influenced the research framework of this study proved insufficient in suggesting determining factors of the MTS and how they generate the four integrating conditions. Contingency factors such as number of locations or employees of the MTS, requirements uncertainty or task dependencies did not determine the way in which the studied MTS established the integrating conditions for coordination. This became especially evident in the analysis of the conditions predictability and accountability.

4.2.6 Stereotypes of Multiteam Systems

In order to disentangle the sources of predictability and, on a smaller scale, accountability, other factors needed to be identified. In the data at hand, the enacted configurations and the sequence in which the integrating conditions were established determined groups within the five cases investigated. Particularly, the way in which accountability and predictability were created, either participatory/ autonomous or prescriptive, established subgroups. The second dimension focuses on the point in time when accountability and predictability as well as common understanding were created. The one group established accountability and predictability early on in the coordination process, while the second group focused first on common understanding and later on accountability and predictability (see Fig. 4.37). The following paragraphs give an overview of the four groups identified and characteristics of said groups.

Group 1: Alpha. This group generated accountability and predictability early on in the process, while common understanding was created in later steps (see Fig. 4.34). This is because their planning was strongly based on top-down directives. Work items were centrally assigned to individual teams, which were then tasked with understanding and implementing these items. This planning approach also explains case Alpha's strong use of prescriptive configurations in its generation of predictability and accountability. Furthermore, their problem resolution strategy was escalation-based, which also implies that a central entity must determine how to solve issues.

Group 2: Delta and Epsilon. As in the previous group, group 2 generated accountability and predictability in a prescriptive fashion. Although Delta's planning mode was described as very inclusive, their way of dealing with unexpected situations remained escalation-based and thus mechanistic prescriptive. While Epsilon's planning mode was more decentralized, the strong influence from the CPO and their way of solving issues also revolved around the intervention of a central entity. The main difference to case Alpha lies in the early focus on common understanding in the process. While group 1 created accountability and predictability early, group 2 focused first on the establishment of common understanding and then on accountability and predictability.

Group 3: Beta and Gamma. In this group accountability was created through the enactment of participatory and autonomous configurations. The planning and system setup of both cases were characterized by their involvement of the teams in decisions and particularly in planning activities. As such, accountability was also created in these coordination configurations where planning occurred. Predictability was mostly created in organic autonomous configurations. The two MTSs in this cluster relied heavily on decentral team PO interaction to exchange information concerning delivery of backlog items. Furthermore, the shorter sprint length of these two cases may have influenced the predilection of this configuration, as it can operate faster. Decentral communication between teams is more flexible and reactive as the enactment of a mechanistic configuration involves a central entity, which reduces reaction speed because more actors are involved.

Group 4: This group remained empty in the five cases investigated in this research. While the combination of dimensions in this group remains theoretically possible, the likelihood of a participatory and autonomous creation of accountability and predictability together with an early focus on both mentioned integrating conditions is less likely. If an MTS exhibits participatory traits it is much more likely that the teams coming together to discuss work items or topics are first going to focus their communication on building a common understanding before deciding who is accountable and how to achieve predictability.

References

Barlow, J. B., Giboney, J. S., Keith, M. J., Wilson, D. W., & Schuetzler, R. M. (2011). Overview and guidance on agile development in large organizations. *Communications of the Association for Information Systems, 29*(2), 25–44.

Hogg, R. V., & Tanis, E. A. (1996). *Probability and statistical inference* (5th ed.). Prentice Hall.

Larman, C., & Vodde, B. (2008). *Scaling lean & agile development: Thinking and organizational tools for large-scale scrum.* Upper Saddle River, N.J: Addison-Wesley Professional.

Larman, C., & Vodde, B. (2010). *Practices for scaling lean and agile development: Large, multisite, and offshore product development with large-scale scrum* (1st ed.). Upper Saddle River, N.J: Addison-Wesley Professional.

Okhuysen, G. A., & Bechky, B. A. (2009). Coordination in organizations: An integrative perspective. *The Academy of Management Annals, 3*(1), 463–502.

Schnackenberg, A. K., & Tomlinson, E. C. (2014). Organizational transparency: A new perspective on managing trust in organization-stakeholder relationships. *Journal of Management*, Advance online publication. Retrieved from http://jom.sagepub.com/content/early/2014/03/06/0149206314525202.abstract

Chapter 5
Discussion and Summary

The last chapter of this dissertation starts with a discussion of the findings in light of the posed research questions. The theoretical and practical contributions are then followed by the limitations of this research as well as the avenues for future work. The chapter finishes with a conclusion.

5.1 Summary of the Findings

This study is in line with previous work on the integrating conditions for coordinated action (e.g Okhuysen and Bechky 2009). It advances this understanding by taking a time-dependent view of the interplay between coordination type, locus and direction as well as how these lead to the integrating conditions for coordinated action. In the section that follows, the research questions that guided this study are recapped and corresponding answers are outlined.

The overarching research question 'How do changes in the coordination configuration affect the integrating conditions for coordination in multiteam software development systems?' was broken down into two specific questions. With this approach, the main research question is answered exhaustively by first answering the two more specific questions.

(1) **Why does the coordination configuration change?**

The study results (see Chap. 4) show that the identification of a deficiency in the integrating conditions present, leads to a change in the coordination configuration. The analysis of 66 interviews resulted in 20 change processes that involved a change in the enacted coordination configuration. The data illustrates that a triggering event in the coordination between two or more teams leads to the identification of an insufficient state concerning the integrating conditions for coordinated action. This realization in turn leads to a change in the enacted coordination configuration in order to establish the missing integrating conditions (see Fig. 5.1).

© Springer International Publishing AG 2017
A. Scheerer, *Coordination in Large-Scale Agile Software Development*,
Progress in IS, DOI 10.1007/978-3-319-55327-6_5

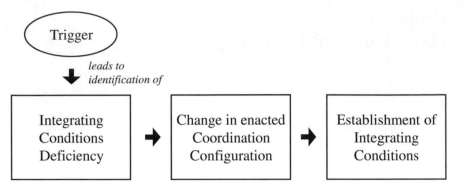

Fig. 5.1 Process leading to a change in the coordination configuration

All processes were provoked by the absence of one or several of the integrating conditions. However, the participants of the coordination process were seldom aware of the underlying factors that were missing. Based on Poole et al. (2000) two causal forces were identified in the data, one that operates continuously and the other that only comes into play at specific points in time. The discrete exogenous trigger is of a distinct nature and can be attributed to a specific point in time (see Fig. 4.7). The second type is the latent endogenous trigger, a more slow moving cause which is of a latent nature and builds up over time until a threshold is reached whence it acts to trigger a change (Grzymala-Busse 2010) (see Fig. 4.11).

(2) **How are the integrating conditions for coordination attained?**

This research shows, that through the enactment of specific coordination configurations, the integrating conditions for coordinated action can be (re-)attained. Based on the previously mentioned processes, six unique configurations in which one of the integrating conditions was established were identified.

In all instances, *transparency* was created in an organic autonomous configuration, as only the teams themselves can choose to intentionally share information (see Sect. 4.1.1.1 for a definition of the term 'transparency'). The integrating condition *common understanding* was established in organic autonomous and organic participatory configurations. Both configurations exhibit an organic coordination mechanism, which supports the formation of a shared understanding through communication.

The integrating conditions *accountability* and *predictability* exhibit distinct variations in how they were constituted. From the empirical data, the five investigated cases showed three groups which differed along two dimensions, namely the prescriptive or participatory nature of accountability and predictability creation and the order in which the integrating conditions common understanding and accountability and predictability were established in the coordination configuration change process (see Sect. 4.2.5). Group 1 generated accountability and predictability early on in the process within prescriptive configurations, while common understanding was created in later steps (see Fig. 4.34). This is because their planning was strongly based on top-down directives, with work items being centrally assigned to individual teams, which were then tasked with understanding and implementing these items. Group 2 established accountability and predictability in a prescriptive fashion as well. The main difference to group 1, i.e. case Alpha, lies in the early focus on common understanding in the process. In group 3 accountability was created through the enactment of participatory and autonomous configurations. The planning and system setup of both cases was characterized by their involvement of the teams in decisions and particularly in planning activities. As such, accountability was also created in these coordination configurations where planning occurred. Predictability was mostly created in organic autonomous configurations.

In summary, the main research question, 'How do changes in the coordination configuration affect integrating conditions in multiteam software development systems' can be answered with: the perception of an imbalance or absence in the integrating conditions for coordinated action leads to a change in the coordination configuration in order to (re)establish said condition(s).

5.2   Theoretical Contributions

The findings of this study contribute to the two main research areas indicated in the introduction: large-scale agile software development and inter-team coordination. As for the first area, the contributions are manifold. First, this research enhances our comprehension of coordination in large-scale software development systems by deriving three particular stereotypes of coordination in these settings from the data. The underlying two dimensions of these types are the prescriptive or participatory nature of accountability and predictability creation and the order in which the integrating conditions common understanding and accountability and predictability were established in the coordination configuration change process (see Sect. 4.2.5). Second, this study improves the understanding of different scaling approaches within large-scale agile software development. It carefully carves out and abstracts the five different practical approaches, namely scaling via Central Team Directives, Central Team Planning based on Team Inputs, Ad Hoc Communication, Iterative Proxy Collaboration and via Full Collaboration (see Sect. 4.1). Contributions to the field of inter-team coordination comprise an improved understanding of how integrating conditions for coordinated action in multiteam systems are established. Furthermore, the integrating conditions were extended with transparency as a fourth dimension. Finally, and most importantly, the conducted research contributes to the integration of the two research fields, by using the lens of inter-team coordination in large-scale agile settings. Doing so, both the established framework as well as the very detailed insights into coordination processes in multiteam systems lead to a better understanding of coordination in large-scale agile software development settings.

Introducing Stereotypes of Coordination in Large-Scale Agile Settings
By grouping the five investigated cases along two dimensions, four groups were generated (see Fig. 4.37). The prescriptive or participatory nature of accountability and predictability creation and the order in which the integrating conditions common understanding and accountability and predictability were established in the coordination configuration change process (see Sect. 4.2.5) are the underlying aspects of this grouping. Of the four possible groups, three could be populated with the cases examined in this research. The unpopulated one seems less likely to be discernible in practice, as the simultaneous focus on early accountability and predictability generation paired with a participatory creation of said integrating conditions does not appear to be an intuitive combination. The participatory nature would most likely lead to the creation of common understanding in a first step and not the other two integrating conditions. These findings contribute to the research stream on large-scale agile software development (cf. Hole and Moe 2008; Lagerberg et al. 2013; Paasivaara et al. 2012).

Better Understanding of Scaling Approaches in Large Agile Software Development
The topic of scaling agile development methods to larger settings has mainly been the focus of practitioner books and frameworks (Ambler and Lines 2012; Larman and Vodde, n.d., 2008, 2010; Leffingwell, n.d.). The amount of published scientific papers on this topic remains scarce (e.g. Lee 2008; Paasivaara et al. 2012; Paasivaara and Lassenius 2011; Smits and Pshigoda 2007). This study has identified how each of the five cases scaled agile practices, either via central team directives, iterative proxy collaboration, central team planning based on team inputs, full collaboration or via ad hoc communication (see Sect. 4.1). By illustrating and explaining the way each of the five cases tried to scale agile methods within its multiteam system, this research contributes to the discussion on large-scale agile development, which until now, followed a mostly normative approach through practitioner guidance (Larman and Vodde 2015; Leffingwell, n.d.).

Advancement and Better Understanding of Integrating Conditions for Coordination
This study contributes to literature that has analyzed the underlying aspects of coordination. In particular, it adds to work that proposed *integrating conditions* for *coordinated action* (Okhuysen and Bechky 2009). Previous publications on coordination can be divided into literature that focused on the decomposition of work (e.g Taylor 1911) and a stream dedicated to the design of work systems, e.g. the specification of coordination structures, mechanisms and strategies (e.g. Espinosa et al. 2004; Li and Maedche 2012; Mintzberg 1983; Thompson 1967). Both streams focus either on teams or on organizations and neglect the more recent multiteam systems form of organizational setup. This study goes beyond these two streams by disentangling the coordination processes between teams. It explains coordination from a process theoretic view and shows how the integrating conditions for coordination are created. The establishment of the four integrating conditions,

transparency, common understanding, accountability and predictability, through the enactment of six coordination configurations (see Fig. 4.30), two organic autonomous ones, an organic participatory, a mechanistic participatory, a mechanistic prescriptive and an organic prescriptive configuration, is one key finding of this study. The enactment of specific coordination configurations to establish certain integrating conditions contributes to a stream of research analyzing the underlying aspects of coordination (cf. Okhuysen and Bechky 2009). By developing a coordination configuration framework, this work allows the visualization and analysis of changes in inter-team coordination and contributes to the stream of research dedicated to the design of work systems (cf. Espinosa et al. 2004; Li and Maedche 2012; Mintzberg 1983; Thompson 1967).

This research contributes to Okhuysen and Bechky's (2009) work by extending the integrating conditions for coordination with *transparency* as a fourth condition. In large-scale software development systems, the possibility to gather an overview of other teams and their state of affairs is essential. As teams are more empowered and gain autonomy, they need to start intentionally sharing correct and relevant information concerning their status or other aspects that could affect surrounding teams. This allows teams within the same multiteam system to anticipate changes and reduces unexpected issues. So far only Dabbish et al. (2014) have associated transparency with coordination. However, the context of their work is situated in the open source community, which exhibits fundamental differences in organizational structure and coordination. The study at hand is one of the first empirical works utilizing the notion of integrating conditions for coordination. In doing so, it can be viewed as a confirmation of the integrating conditions by Okhuysen and Bechky (2009).

Aptness of Embedded Information Systems Development Research
This study would not have been possible in its current form without the opportunities given in the context of an embedded research project. Due to the complex nature of large-scale software development, such an inside view of development systems was invaluable as it allowed for a deep understanding of the context and the underlying influencing factors. Furthermore, the possibility to investigate several multiteam systems was profoundly supported by the size and accessibility within the larger organization. The synergy of academia and industry allowed this research to evolve in a highly relevant way for theory and practice.

Future researchers in the IS domain should consider a similar setup. It allows the contemplation of processes and methods apart from the daily business, where often enough a long-term reflective view, oriented towards understanding, explaining and advancing key elements of the work process, falls behind in relation to more pressing short term topics. In doing so, researchers can advance their theoretical understanding of phenomena while arousing interest from large software development organizations by consulting and advising on the topics under study.

5.3 Practical Contributions

Coordination in large-scale agile software development systems is a highly relevant topic for practitioners. As bigger and more complex software is being developed in an agile manner, the need to understand inter-team coordination is essential.

Agile and especially large-scale agile development constitutes a structural change in the organization and needs concurrent change management and continuous improvement to develop according to the given context it is deployed in. The range of agile methods, techniques and advice is enormous and each adoption customizes the textbook approaches to their needs. Most literature on large-scale agile is of a normative nature originating from consultants wishing to promote their work. It is here that this study provides evidence as to how agile has been scaled in real life settings and can act as a foundation of evidence-based management of software products (Boehm and Lane 2010; Dybå et al. 2005). This permits leaders to base their decisions on factual evidence rather than anecdotal narratives and allows managers to perform their jobs better by employing a deeper logic to the explanation of what works and what does not.

The interest in agile and especially in large-scale agile software development is mounting across the industry (VersionOne Inc 2012; West et al. 2010). The company-wide introduction of agile methods at SAP SE confirms the high interest of large organizations to take advantage of agile development. However, as both shown in this study and Schmidt (2016) the adoption of such methods is accompanied by a significant cultural change. The manageable act of introducing agile methods into software development processes is not enough. A continuous effort to transform the organization is needed. As such, aspects such as scaling agile methods to larger settings and the adjustment of said methods to the organizational environment at hand necessitate a long-term change management, which practitioners need to be aware of before deciding to go down this path.

The results provide practitioners with a guideline to evaluate coordination practices in large-scale agile development settings. Based on the four integrating conditions for coordination from this study, transparency, common understanding, accountability and predictability, decision makers such as Scrum Masters or Product Owners, and other agile leaders can assess if currently employed coordination practices contribute to these conditions and lead to the intended results. By focusing on common understanding and transparency for example, Scrum Masters can evaluate if proposed large-scale practices such as the Scrum of Scrums practice is the right choice for their environment and if it is generating the intended results. In multiteam systems, integrating conditions such as common understanding are increasingly difficult to establish as compared to small settings. Therefore, agile coaches and Scrum Masters need to pay special attention to practices that create this condition early on, such as joint release planning with all involved roles for the next release (e.g. product owners, product managers, etc.). Furthermore, the integrating conditions can act as a guide in developing coordination structures for future multiteam systems by explicating clear goals of what to strive for in the coordination of agile software development multiteam systems, specifically transparency, common understanding, accountability and predictability.

5.4 Limitations of the Study and Future Research

The embedded nature of this study allowed for unique access and a rare opportunity to study large-scale development systems in the field. Simply put, this research would not have been possible from an outside perspective. The possibility to identify appropriate cases for this study, talk informally with any colleague, gather data in the form of large interview studies or have access to project management systems, are just a few of the advantages of this setting. However, some drawbacks due to the nature of this approach had to be accepted. While participants stemmed from 11 locations in five countries, all belonged to one organization developing enterprise systems. This controls for inter-firm differences in that contextual factors originating from different organizational settings are minimized. However, due to the focus on one organization, the results of this study may be limited in their generalizability, as the contextual environment is likely to differ in other firms. Furthermore, the author's embeddedness may have led to a biased perspective, as context-specific characteristics and phenomena may have been overrated or not considered. However, this bias was controlled by continuous discussions with colleagues in academia and other professional software development organizations.

Although an accepted data gathering and analysis process with a second coder was followed until consensus was reached, the assessment of conditions and mechanisms may show biases due to subjective ratings. Additionally, because of the large-scale nature of this research, it was necessary to interview numerous people per case. Starting with the Chief Product Owner all the way to each team Product Owner and many Scrum Masters as well as additional roles led to a thorough penetration of each case. On the one hand this mitigated a key informant bias (Kumar et al. 1993) but on the other did not allow for a great amount of cases to be investigated. Future research should therefore investigate this study's topic in varied settings. Different types of software under development and in particular different organizational cultures would be of great interest.

As this study can be regarded as a first foray into coordination in large-scale agile development systems, future research can delve more deeply into particular aspects of this study. As such, this study distinguished two categories of inter-team dependencies. With the ongoing interest in different team compositions, e.g. feature teams, multiteam systems employing such a composition may exhibit different types of dependencies. An interesting line of inquiry might be the differentiation of more dependencies categories, e.g. knowledge dependencies (Faraj and Sproull 2000; Strode et al. 2012), between teams and their impact on the multiteam system.

This study revealed certain enacted coordination configurations as a precursor to particular established integrating conditions. However, no assertion can be made to the necessity of the occurrence of all integrating conditions. The process level investigated showed several processes that established only three or fewer conditions. One possible explanation might be that the other conditions were already present in the larger environment surrounding the processes. Future studies may examine this relation and how it affects a threshold that might be present for the integrating conditions to lead to coordinated action.

In line with this train of thought, the interplay of integrating conditions and how these conditions influence the establishment of coordinated action is another promising area. Future research may investigate if all integrating conditions are necessary to achieve coordinated action or even if some conditions can substitute others.

The findings of this study showed large differences between multiteam systems concerning their development and planning cycle. Especially between cases Alpha and Beta, these distinctions were obvious. Their current general coordination style may be deeply rooted in their product structure, which may have influenced their organizational structure as well (cf. Colfer and Baldwin 2010; Conway 1968; MacCormack et al. 2008). Such an inquiry seems particularly promising to investigate more closely the relationship between product structure and organizational structure and its impact on coordination between teams.

5.5 Summary

The introduction of agile software development methods in the 1990s has had a profound effect on the way software is being developed today. Originally promoted by consultants and practitioners, early evidence from industry seemed promising. Over the years, agile development methods have gained widespread acceptance and have become the de facto standard in large parts of the industry (VersionOne Inc 2013; West et al. 2010). The last decade has seen an increase in research concerning agile development, however a theoretical understanding is still in its infancy (Dybå and Dingsøyr 2008). As the acceptance of agile has spread, so too has the interest of large organizations to benefit from the promoted advantages these development methods have to offer. However, large-scale settings with several development teams (multiteam systems), often including 50 people and more, pose a very different challenge than small team settings (cf. Dingsøyr et al. 2014). The coordination of these higher number of teams and people becomes an increasingly difficult task, which has led to a call for research on inter-team coordination in large-scale agile development (Dingsøyr and Moe 2013, 2014). The study at hand, answers this call through a qualitative process-theoretic multiple case study. It examined five multiteam systems in a real-life industry setting at SAP SE.

Based on a thorough review of the literature on coordination in organizational science, teamwork cognition and previous work in the field of agile development, a preliminary research framework was constructed. This framework was then refined through interview data to act as the foundation for the analysis of coordination processes in large-scale agile development systems. The framework consists of a coordination configuration with the dimensions coordination type, locus and direction and integrating conditions for coordinated action in the form of transparency, common understanding, accountability and predictability. The integrating conditions for coordination are established by enacting specific coordination configurations that are a composite of the just mentioned dimensions within the configuration. The study resulted in 58 hours of recorded interviews summing up to 1100 pages of transcribed data. The 66 interviewees belonged to five different product development programs each consisting of four to 13 teams.

Overall, 20 processes of inter-team coordination were identified, each leading to a change in the integrating conditions for coordinated action. Based on this empirical evidence several key findings emerged. The data illustrates that a triggering event in the coordination between two or more teams leads to the identification of an insufficient state concerning the integrating conditions for coordinated action. This realization in turn leads to a change in the enacted coordination configuration in order to establish the missing integrating conditions. Based on the previously mentioned processes, this study identified six unique configurations in which one of the integrating conditions was established. Another key finding of this study was revealed in the cross-case analysis. Namely, it exposed three stereotypes of multiteam systems based on the prescriptive or participatory nature of accountability and predictability creation and the order in which the integrating conditions common understanding and accountability and predictability were established in the coordination configuration change process (see Sect. 4.2.5). The research unveiled different scaling approaches of the examined multiteam systems and showed that the participatory or prescriptive nature of coordination was determined by the approach chosen to scale agile methods to the respective multiteam setting.

This study contributes to a better understanding of coordination in large-scale agile development settings by disentangling the coordination processes between teams. It explains coordination from a process theoretic view and shows how the integrating conditions for coordination are established. It advances the notion of integrating conditions for coordination by presenting empirical evidence and extends these conditions by introducing transparency as fourth condition. This research contributes to practice by showing evidence of real life scaling of agile methods in a field setting. The results provide a guideline to practitioners on how to evaluate large-scale coordination efforts and underline the continuous effort needed to promote agile methods in these settings as the introduction of these methods necessitates a cultural change.

Future research should build on the presented insights and expand upon them to gain a deeper understanding of inter-team coordination in large-scale agile settings.

References

Ambler, S. W., & Lines, M. (2012). *Disciplined agile delivery: A practitioner's guide to agile software delivery in the enterprise*. IBM Press.

Boehm, B., & Lane, J. A. (2010). Evidence-based software processes. In J. Münch, Y. Yang, & W. Schäfer (Eds.), *New modeling concepts for today's software processes* (Vol. 6195, pp. 62–73). Berlin, Heidelberg: Springer. Retrieved from http://dx.doi.org/10.1007/978-3-642-14347-2_7

Colfer, L., & Baldwin, C. Y. (2010). *The mirroring hypothesis: Theory, evidence and exceptions* (No. 10-058). *Harvard Business School*.

Conway, M. E. (1968). How do committees invent. *Datamation, 14*(4), 28–31.

Dabbish, L., Stuart, C., Tsay, J., & Herbsleb, J. D. (2014). Transparency and coordination in peer production. Retrieved from http://arxiv.org/abs/1407.0377

Dingsøyr, T., Fægri, T. E., & Itkonen, J. (2014). What is large in large-scale? A taxonomy of scale for agile software development. In A. Jedlitschka, P. Kuvaja, M. Kuhrmann, T. Männistö, J. Münch, & M. Raatikainen (Eds.), *Product-focused software process improvement* (Vol. 8892, pp. 273–276). Springer International Publishing. Retrieved from http://link.springer.com/10.1007/978-3-319-13835-0

Dingsøyr, T., & Moe, N. B. (2013). Research challenges in large-scale agile software development. *ACM SIGSOFT Software Engineering Notes, 38*(5), 38–39. Retrieved from http://dl.acm.org/citation.cfm?id=2507288.2507322

Dingsøyr, T., & Moe, N. B. (2014). Towards principles of large-scale agile development. In T. Dingsøyr, N. Moe, R. Tonelli, S. Counsell, C. Gencel, & K. Petersen (Eds.), *Agile methods. Large-scale development, refactoring, testing, and estimation* (Vol. 199, pp. 1–8). Springer International Publishing. Retrieved from http://www.springer.com/computer/swe/book/978-3-319-14357-6

Dybå, T., & Dingsøyr, T. (2008). Empirical studies of agile software development: A systematic review. *Information and Software Technology, 50*(9–10), 833–859. Retrieved from http://linkinghub.elsevier.com/retrieve/pii/S0950584908000256

Dybå, T., Kitchenham, B. A., & Jorgensen, M. (2005). Evidence-based software engineering for practitioners. *IEEE Software, 22*(1), 58–65.

Espinosa, J. A., Lerch, J. F., Kraut, R. E., Salas, E., & Fiore, S. M. (2004). Explicit vs. implicit coordination mechanisms and task dependencies: One size does not fit all. In *Team cognition: Understanding the factors that drive process and performance.* (pp. 107–129). Washington, DC: American Psychological Association.

Faraj, S., & Sproull, L. (2000). Coordinating expertise in software development teams. *Management Science, 46*(12), 1554–1568. Retrieved from http://www.jstor.org/stable/2661533

Grzymala-Busse, A. (2010). Time will tell? Temporality and the analysis of causal mechanisms and processes. *Comparative Political Studies, 44*(9), 1267–1297. Retrieved from http://cps.sagepub.com/content/44/9/1267

Hole, S., & Moe, N. B. (2008). A case study of coordination in distributed agile software development. In R. O'Connor, N. Baddoo, K. Smolander, & R. Messnarz (Eds.), *Software process improvement* (Vol. 16, pp. 189–200). Berlin, Heidelberg: Springer. Retrieved from http://dx.doi.org/10.1007/978-3-540-85936-9_17

Kumar, N., Stern, L. W., & Anderson, J. C. (1993). Conducting interorganizational research using key informants. *Academy of Management Journal, 36*(6), 1633–1651.

Lagerberg, L., Skude, T., Emanuelsson, P., Sandahl, K., & Stahl, D. (2013). The impact of agile principles and practices on large-scale software development projects: A multiple-case study of two projects at Ericsson. In *International Symposium on Empirical Software Engineering and Measurement* (pp. 348–356).

Larman, C., & Vodde, B. (2008). *Scaling lean & agile development: Thinking and organizational tools for large-scale scrum*. Upper Saddle River, N.J: Addison-Wesley Professional.

Larman, C., & Vodde, B. (2010). *Practices for scaling lean and agile development: Large, multisite, and offshore product development with large-scale scrum* (1st ed.). Upper Saddle River, N.J.: Addison-Wesley Professional.

Larman, C., & Vodde, B. (2015). *Large-scale scrum: More with LeSS*. Addison-Wesley Professional.

Lee, E. C. (2008). Forming to performing: Transitioning large-scale project into agile. In *AGILE Conference* (pp. 106–111). Los Alamitos, CA, USA: IEEE Computer Society.

Leffingwell, D. (n.d.). Scaled agile framework. Retrieved from http://www.scaledagileframework.com/

Li, Y., & Maedche, A. (2012). Formulating effective coordination strategies in agile global software development teams. In *Proceedings of the International Conference on Information Systems (ICIS 2012)* (pp. 1–6).

MacCormack, A., Baldwin, C. Y., & Rusnak, J. (2008). Exploring the duality between product and organizational architectures: A test of the "mirroring" hypothesis. *Research Policy, 41*(8), 1309–1324.

Mintzberg, H. (1983). *Structure in fives: Designing effective organizations*. Prentice-Hall, Inc. Retrieved from http://psycnet.apa.org/psycinfo/1992-98280-000.

Okhuysen, G. A., & Bechky, B. A. (2009). Coordination in organizations: An integrative perspective. *The Academy of Management Annals, 3*(1), 463–502.

Paasivaara, M., & Lassenius, C. (2011). Scaling scrum in a large distributed project. In *Empirical Software Engineering and Measurement (ESEM), 2011 International Symposium on* (pp. 363–367).

Paasivaara, M., Lassenius, C., & Heikkila, V. T. (2012). Inter-team coordination in large-scale globally distributed scrum: Do Scrum-of-Scrums really work? In *Empirical Software Engineering and Measurement (ESEM), 2012 ACM-IEEE International Symposium on* (pp. 235–238).

Poole, M. S., Van De Ven, A. H., Dooley, K., & Holmes, M. E. (2000). *Organizational change and innovation processes: Theory and methods for research. Organizational change and innovation processes theory and methods for research*. Oxford University Press.

Schmidt, C. (2016). *Agile software development teams*. Springer International Publishing.

Smits, H., & Pshigoda, G. (2007). Implementing scrum in a distributed software development organization. In *Agile Conference (AGILE), 2007* (pp. 371–375).

Strode, D. E., Huff, S. L., Hope, B., & Link, S. (2012). Coordination in co-located agile software development projects. *Journal of Systems and Software, 85*(6), 1222–1238. Retrieved from http://dx.doi.org/10.1016/j.jss.2012.02.017

Taylor, F. W. (1911). *The principles of scientific management*. New York, London: Harper & Brothers.

Thompson, J. D. (1967). *Organizations in action: Social science bases of administrative theory* (Vol. 48). New York: McGraw-Hill.

VersionOne Inc. (2012). 7th annual state of agile development survey. Retrieved from http://www.versionone.com/pdf/7th-Annual-State-of-Agile-Development-Survey.pdf

VersionOne Inc. (2013). 8th annual state of agile development survey. Retrieved from www.versionone.com/pdf/2013-state-of-agile-survey.pdf

West, D., Grant, T., Gerush, M., & D'Silva, D. (2010). Agile development: Mainstream adoption has changed agility. *Forrester Research*.

Erratum to: Coordination in Large-Scale Agile Software Development

Alexander Scheerer

Erratum to:
A. Scheerer, *Coordination in Large-Scale Agile Software Development*, Progress in IS, DOI 10.1007/978-3-319-55327-6

In the original version of the book, in Copyright page (p. iv) of the front matter, the sentence "This book is based on a doctoral thesis successfully defended at the Business School of the University of Mannheim" should be added and also the table in "Appendix B Coding Schemes" is to be formatted as two tables in p. 124. The erratum book has been updated with the changes.

The updated original online version for this book can be found at
DOI 10.1007/978-3-319-55327-6

© Springer International Publishing AG 2017
A. Scheerer, *Coordination in Large-Scale Agile Software Development*,
Progress in IS, DOI 10.1007/978-3-319-55327-6_6

Appendix

A   Interview Guideline

Introduction Discussion Partners

1. Joint Research project between Mannheim University and SAP
2. Scientific research on coordination in large scale agile development systems.
3. Ensuring anonymity and approval of interview recording.

Background Questions

4. We would like to know more about you and your work. Could you provide us with your background and roughly introduce your tasks?

   a. *What is your role/your responsibilities?*
   b. *What professional experience and educational background do you have?*

5. How long have you been working for SAP?

   a. *Within this product area?*
   b. *In this team?*

Project Characteristics

6. What software are you developing?
7. How long has this product been in existence?
8. When did the current release start?
9. What is the status of the release?
10. How long are your sprints?
11. How often do you deliver to the customer?
12. How long are the planning cycles (Waves) in your program?
13. Would you describe the coordination within your unit as rather bottom up or top down?

© Springer International Publishing AG 2017
A. Scheerer, *Coordination in Large-Scale Agile Software Development*,
Progress in IS, DOI 10.1007/978-3-319-55327-6

14. How would you characterize the project?

    a. Complexity
    b. Uncertainty

15. How novel are the tasks?

    a. Technological novelty of the outcome
    b. novelty related to the working methods used in the program
    c. novelty of the resource and competence needs in the program

16. How analyzable are the tasks of the project

    a. working methods are well-known
    b. resource and competence needs understood and defined
    c. clarity about inter-project interdependencies
    d. clarity about relevant stakeholders

Team and MTS Characteristics

17. How many teams are involved in the project?
18. What is the average number of members of a team?
19. What kind of tasks are done by your team

    a. New development
    b. Enhancements of existing functionalities
    c. Support
    d. Bug fixing

20. How do you report progress?
21. How do you communicate beside the official channels?
22. How are the teams structured?

    a. *Are the teams either component or feature based?*
    b. *With which team you collaborate the most? Which team do you dependon the most?*
    c. *What kind of dependencies exist between the mentioned teams?*
    d. *Are there changes over time?*
    e. *Does this collaboration work well?*

23. How autonomous are the single teams?

    a. *Can they choose development techniques by themselves?*
    b. *Can they influence the backlog?*

Technical Characteristics

24. Which programming languages do you use?
25. How yo do you integrate code?

    a. *Continuous integration*
    b. *ABAP transports*

26. How do you test, which type of tests do you use?

    a. *unit tests, integration tests*
    b. *Selenium*
    c. *Scenario tests*

27. How do you validate?

    a. *takt based validation*
    b. *Validation at the end of the release*

Context Characteristics

28. How is your team embedded into the organization?

    a. Dependencies to other departments

29. Do the teams work in different locations?

    a. *Which locations?*
    b. *How do you communicate with these teams?*

30. What effects follow from this separation?

    a. Time differences
    b. lack of critical task awareness

31. Are the teams similar in terms of problem solving, decision making and coordination processes?

32. What problems do you encounter when trying to communicate, coordinate, or exchange information with other teams?

    a. *Locally*
    b. *With other sites*

33. How are these problems addressed, or how could they be addressed effectively?

    a. *Locally*
    b. *With other sites ?*

34. How are coordination activities like Scrum meetings conducted with teams in different locations?

    a. Synchronous communication tools (online meeting, ...)
    b. Asynchronous communication tools (wiki, email, ...)

35. What were, in your opinion, the main coordination challenges in regard to

    a. *Temporal differences*
    b. *Geographic distance*
    c. *Cultural differences and language differences*

Coordination Mechanisms

36. How much project understanding is needed?

    a. in order to develop it
    b. in order to coordinate the teams?

37. Who is responsible for the coordination

    a. *Between teams?*
    b. *In your team?*

38. How are backlog items distributed to single teams?

    a. *What kind of planning is used?*

        1. *Regular meetings*
        2. *Open discussions*
        3. *Fixed planning*

39. How are dependencies between teams managed?
40. What are typical reasons/causes for/sources for dependencies between teams?
41. Which mechanisms and activities do you think are especially helpful? What makes them so helpful?
42. What technologies are used?

    a. *For coordination*
    b. *For Communication*

43. How do you improve your processes?
44. Where do you get information regarding skills and knowledge of your colleagues?

    a. *From where do you know who you have to contact if you have problems/questions?*

45. What are in your opinion necessary requirements for good coordination?

Coordination-Effectiveness

46. How would you describe the coordination effectiveness of this product?

    a. *Was it overall a well-coordinated or problematic coordinated project?*
    b. *What are the reasons for this evaluation?*

47. Please imagine a situation where you collaborated with another team and the coordination between the teams was not effective.

    a. Could you give us a detailed description?

        1. *Who was involved?*
        2. *When did it occur?*

    b. *How often did such situations occur?*
    c. *Why was it not effective?*
    d. *How was the situation solved?*

48. Please imagine a situation for the same context, where coordination between the teams was very effective.

    a. Could you give us a detailed description?

        (i) *Who was involved?*
        (ii). *When did it occur?*

    b. *How often did such situations occur?*
    c. *What was different regarding the previous situation?*

49. Based on your past experience, when are teams well-coordinated?
50. What would help you coordinate better?
51. What are best practices or lessons learned which you could recommend to other programs?

Conversation closer

Did we forget to talk about any aspects of inter-team coordination?

B   Coding Schemes

Construct	Values	Coding scheme	Examples
Product complexity	Low	The product was easy to develop and understand	–
	Low-medium	The software required very little technical or business domain knowledge and was straightforward to implement	–
	Medium	An average technical or business domain knowledge is necessary. A developer can become acquainted with both in a reasonable time frame	"It is of average complexity"
	Medium-high	The product exhibits an above average need for specific business domain or technical knowledge. A few weeks time are needed for developers to become acquainted with the product	–

(continued)

(continued)

Construct	Values	Coding scheme	Examples
	High	A developer needs several months to grasp all the facets of the product. High business domain knowledge or technical expertis is needed to develop the product	"It is the highest level of orchestration" "It is a very configurable product and therefore highly complex"
Requirements Uncertainty	Low	Requirements are defined and do not change	"We have stable requirements"
	Low-medium	Software requirements are defined and do not change very often over the course of development	"They haven't changed much" "The requirements don't change that fast"
	Medium	Requirements can change in development on a more regular basis and developers need to clarify questions regarding the requirements	"Even as we get into the development there are still open questions"
	Medium-high	The requirements exhibit a lack of detail and almost all of them need clarification. Requirements change from time to time in the development phase	"The backlog items we get are rather coarse grained"
	High	New Requirements arrive on a constant basis and are very broadly described	"We constantly get new requirements"

Construct	Values	Coding scheme
Coordination Type	Mechanistic	Plan, rules, regulations or roles were used as mechanisms
	Organic	Communication, mutual adjustment and feedback was utilised
Coordination Locus	Centralized	A central team or central superior is in charge of coordination
	Decentralized	Employees on the same hierarchical level are in charge of coordination decisions
Coordination Direction	Vertical	Communication across hierarchical levels is necessary for coordination
	Horizontal	Communication on the same hierarchical level is necessary for coordination

(continued)

(continued)

Construct	Values	Coding scheme
Dependencies	Sequential	Backlog items are dependent on an item from another team. One team consumes from another team. A team delivers an item to another team
	Reciprocal	Collaborative working style between two teams. They have to work closely together and must simultaneously implement requirements

C Network Analysis Results

Graph parameter	Alpha	Beta	Gamma	Delta	Epsilon
# Strongly connected components	5	3	5	3	2
Average degree	2.692	3.111	2.143	1.667	1.500
Density	0.231	0.389	0.357	0.333	0.500
Diameter	5	3	2	3	1

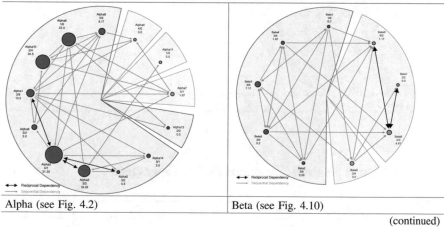

Alpha (see Fig. 4.2)	Beta (see Fig. 4.10)

(continued)

(continued)

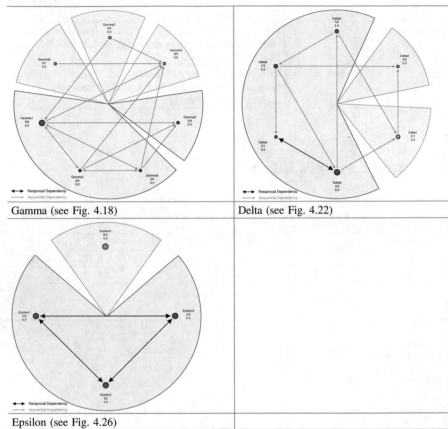

Gamma (see Fig. 4.18)

Delta (see Fig. 4.22)

Epsilon (see Fig. 4.26)

D   Multiteam System Characteristics Overview

	Alpha	Beta	Gamma	Delta	Epsilon
Teams	13	9	7	6	4
Locations	4	2	6	1	3
Employees	~140	~95	~50	~85	~40
Avg. Company Tenure (years)	12	11	12	18	13

(continued)

(continued)

	Alpha	Beta	Gamma	Delta	Epsilon
Avg. MTS Tenure (years)	5	4	5	2	7
Product type	On-premise	Cloud	On-premise and cloud	On-premise	On-premise and cloud
Product complexity	High	Medium-high	Medium-high	High	Medium-high
Requirements uncertainty	Low-medium	Low-medium	Low-medium	Low-medium	Medium-high
High-level planning horizon (months)	Years	3	3	3	3
Customer delivery (months)	12	1	4	3	3
Sprint planning horizon (weeks)	12	4	4	4	4
Sprint length (weeks)	4	2	2	4	4
Product architecture	Highly integrated	Modular	Modular	Integrated	Modular
Product Maturity[a] (years)	>10	>5	>1	>3	>10
Inter-team coordination responsibility	Central team, team product owner	Team product owner, scrum master	Scrum master	Chief product owner, team product owner	Team product owner, team architect

[a]Product Maturity was difficult to specify, as the current products often had precursors which either were consumed in newer solutions or where used as foundation for a new product

E   Process Overview

MTS	ID	Initial ICs				Trigger	Process				Final ICs				Final NCs originating from Configuration			
		Transparency	Common Understanding	Accountability	Predictability		Step 1	Step 2	Step 3	Step 4	Transparency	Common Understanding	Accountability	Predictability	Transparency	Common Understanding	Accountability	Predictability
Alpha	Alpha-P1		○			unclear mutual expectations					○	●	●					
Alpha	Alpha-P2	○	○			lacking knowledge of other team's activities					○	○	●	●				
Alpha	Alpha-P3	○	○			unknown dependencies between teams					○	●						
Alpha	Alpha-P4	●	●	●		increase in geographic dispersion					○	○	○					
Alpha	Alpha-P5			○		corruption of shared codebase							●					
Alpha	Alpha-P6	○	○	○	○	work item spanning across teams					●	●	●	●				
Alpha	Alpha-P7		○	○	○	unclear work items					●	●	○					
Beta	Beta-P1	○			○	Missing communication of decommitment					●			●				
Beta	Beta-P2		○	○		work item spanning across teams					●	●						
Beta	Beta-P3		○			unclear usage of new development framework					●							
Beta	Beta-P4		○			major testing failures of new feature					●		●					
Beta	Beta-P5		○	○	○	new cross team feature originating from team					●	●	●					
Beta	Beta-P6	●	○			prio conflict within takt					●	●	●					
Beta	Beta-P7		○			assumptions mismatch					●							
Delta	Delta-P1			○		competing concept deadlock							●					
Delta	Delta-P2			○	○	unresolved prioritization of topic							●	●				
Delta	Delta-P3	●	○	●		work item spanning across teams with one team lacking knowledge					●	●	●					
Epsilon	Epsilon-P1	●	○	●		recognition of reuse possibility					●	●	●					
Epsilon	Epsilon-P2	○	○	○		discovery of redundancies					●	●	●					
Gamma	Gamma-P1	○			○	late delivery of needed functionality					●			●				
Gamma	Gamma-P2	○	○	○	○	rapid delivery of patch necessary					●	●	●	●				
Gamma	Gamma-P3		○	○	○	work item across teams					●	●	●					

The purpose of the colors in this chart are for better readability.

Printed in the United States
By Bookmasters